EBJ   MDCCCLXXI.

Pre-Raphaelite Women

JAN MARSH

Pre-Raphaelite Women

IMAGES OF FEMININITY IN PRE-RAPHAELITE ART

PHOENIX ILLUSTRATED

Text copyright © Jan Marsh, 1987

First published in 1987 by
George Weidenfeld & Nicolson Ltd

This paperback edition first published in 1998 by
Phoenix Illustrated
Orion Publishing Group,
Orion House,
5, Upper St. Martin's Lane
London WC2H 9EA

British Library Cataloguing-in-Publication Data
A catalogue record for this book is available from
the British Library

ISBN 0753802104

Designed by Mavis Henley

Typeset by Keyspools, Globorne, Lancs
Colour separations by Newsele Litho Limited
Printed and bound by L.E.G.O. Vicenza

Half-title page: Edward Burne-Jones,
Study of Woman's Head (Maria Zambaco), 1871
Title-page: John Everett Millais, *Mariana*, 1851

Contents

Acknowledgements

This book is dedicated to the members of the Victorian Art Research Seminar at the Paul Mellon Centre in London, and to the University of London Women's History Seminar at the Institute of Historical Research, whose papers and discussions have covered a wide range of topics relating to the representation of women in art and history.

Particular thanks are due, as always, to Hilary Morgan and Pat Thane, who with others convene these seminars and whose generous sharing of knowledge has shaped my understanding and analysis relating to the history of women and painting in the nineteenth century. Others who deserve my grateful thanks for assistance and encouragement in the field of Pre-Raphaelite studies include a large number of individuals and institutions, many of whose own works are cited in the Select Bibliography and Notes and References; in the text they will see other examples of their insights and information for which it has not proved possible to give detailed references in a study of this sort, but whose contribution to Pre-Raphaelite scholarship is gratefully acknowledged. They include: Norah Gillow and Peter Cormack, William Morris Gallery, London; Susan P. Casteras, Yale Center for British Art, New Haven; Stephen Wildman and Tessa Sidey, Birmingham Museum and Art Gallery; Mark Haworth-Booth, Victoria and Albert Museum, London; John Christian; Pamela Gerrish Nunn; Jeremy Maas; Judith Bronkhurst; Lynda Nead; Gail Nina Anderson; Tamar Garb; John House; Mrs I. Dennis; Christine Poulson; Ina Taylor; Christopher Wood; and the staff of the Prints and Drawings Department at the Ashmolean Museum, Oxford.

The publishers and I are most grateful to all the galleries, museums and individuals who have kindly either given permission for their pictures to be reproduced, or supplied photographs.

On a wider level, I should also like to thank all professional and personal friends who have encouraged, supported or endured my consuming passion for Pre-Raphaelite women in their various guises.

Introduction

The painting of Pre-Raphaelite women begins with poetry. Key texts from English Romanticism inspired the young artists of the Brotherhood and their associates – texts that recur throughout the period and style of art now known as Pre-Raphaelite.

The first of these poetic texts is John Keats's 'The Eve of St Agnes', with its romantic tale of awakening sexuality and elopement in a faraway dream world. The young hero Porphyro hides in Madeline's bedchamber,

> That he might see her beauty unespied
> And win perhaps that night a peerless bride
> While legion'd fairies paced the coverlet
> And pale enchantment held her sleepy-eyed.

On her lute he plays 'an ancient ditty' called 'La belle dame sans merci' – the title Keats gave to other verses which were to provide painters with a recurrent motif of the fairy enchantress, alluring but heartless, who leaves the knight 'alone and palely loitering . . . On the cold hill side', pining for his cruel lady.

Keats's mantle as poet of love and romance was taken up by Alfred Tennyson, whose haunting 'Lady of Shalott' gave the Pre-Raphaelite artists another, almost obsessional, theme. And in striking contrast to Keats's 'Eve of St Agnes' Tennyson made the heroine of his own 'St Agnes' Eve' not a nubile maiden awaiting a vision of her lover, but a novice nun on a wintry night contemplating her vows:

> The shadows of the convent towers
> Slant down the snowy sward,
> Still creeping with the creeping hours
> That lead me to the Lord.

Together, these images of sexuality and sanctity represent two of the opposed but complementary aspects of womanhood, as defined in the Victorian age, whose variants and influences on life and art form the subject of this book. Woman as desirable, woman as chaste, woman as dutiful, woman as witch: these are among the images that both reflected and shaped the ideas of the age regarding the relations of the sexes and the ideals of masculinity and femininity. Such ideas were powerfully expressed in both painting and poetry, and supported, as we shall see, by the new art of photography, in a collaboration of visual and verbal representation that was a potent force of cultural definition.

3 Dante Gabriel Rossetti, Mariana, 1868–70.

Woman as the subject and inspiration of art is not the only theme in Pre-Raphaelite painting, which also encompassed landscape and portraiture, as well as biblical, historical and heroic themes, and some subjects from contemporary life. But images of women dominate Pre-Raphaelite art – the term is indeed now synonymous with a specific feminine appearance, with loose hair, large eyes, elongated neck and soulful expression – either as depictions of figures from literature and legend, or in symbolic or metaphorical aspect as allegories and personifications of abstract qualities.

It is not easy to account for this preoccupation with the female form except in terms of an underlying obsession with the nature of femininity; clearly, however, it was both influenced by and an influence on the contemporary articulation of ideas about women, at a time when relations between the sexes were, as always, undergoing change, and when the traditional patriarchal social structure was under stress.

The nineteenth century was a period of rapid and immense social and economic change, with corresponding cultural repercussions. Changes in patterns of work and family life, together with the great expansion of the middle and professional classes – the chief patrons of Pre-Raphaelite art – established new structures of feeling and of representation whereby women were both elevated and constrained, worshipped and restricted to specific roles. Framed images of idealized women, displayed on the walls of bourgeois homes and art galleries, were a kind of metaphor for the position ascribed to women in Victorian society.

The profound identification of Art with Woman occurred in both pictorial and personal contexts. This book explores the intricate involvement on all levels of Pre-Raphaelite artists and their female models; here it is important to understand how deeply the relationship between artist and woman extended to all aspects of painting. At its simplest, this is represented by Rose, the heroine of Tennyson's poem 'The Gardener's Daughter', whose beauty inspires both love and art. The narrator is a painter, whose creativity is raised to divine heights by the sight of his beloved tying up an errant bloom, 'one arm aloft':

> . . . the full day dwelt on her brows, and sunn'd
> Her violet eyes . . .
> And on the bounteous wave of such a breast
> As never pencil drew. Half light, half shade,
> She stood . . .

The story ends with the painter unveiling his masterpiece: a picture of Rose, his 'first, last love; the idol of my youth' and 'darling of my manhood'.

The association of girls with flowers is of course traditionally expressive of youthful love and a gently unfolding bliss. Paradise, as the poet Swinburne playfully remarked at the height of his own infatuation with Pre-Raphaelitism, must surely be 'a rosegarden full of stunners'. The link is delineated in dozens of

4 *Julia Margaret Cameron,*
The Gardener's Daughter, *1867.*

5 *Dante Gabriel Rossetti,* The Roseleaf, *1870.*

Victorian pictures, including Rossetti's portrait of Jane Morris in *The Roseleaf* (1870) [5] where the curves of stem and leaves echo those of the model's hand and head. The title of Anna Mary Howitt's *The Sensitive Plant – The Lady* (1855), taken from Shelley, makes explicit the woman-as-flower motif. In the poem:

> She lifted their heads with her tender hands
> And sustained them with rods and osier bands,
> If the flowers had been her own infants, she
> Could never have nursed them more tenderly . . .

The young woman tending the roses in Julia Margaret Cameron's photograph *The Gardener's Daughter* [4], is a simple rendering of the theme, born of Cameron's admiration for Tennyson and all his works. It, too, offers a direct analogy between flowers, feminine beauty and art, with the unspoken refrain that the first two, alas, will fade: art alone has eternal loveliness. The model for the photograph, incidentally, was probably Mary Ryan, a fatherless Irish girl adopted by Julia Margaret Cameron to serve as housemaid and model. A young gentleman fell in love with her portrait in an exhibition and sent his proposal; they married and, according to his memoirs, Mary was his 'devoted companion and helpmeet through many years of vicissitudes and successes, sorrows and aspirations, clouds and sunshine'. [1]

But woman was more than the simple subject and inspiration of art. She represented the artist's own soul, the creative impulse of his art, in an idea repeatedly elaborated in a metaphor of the male artist and his ideal woman. This is spelt out most strikingly in *Hand and Soul*, a very early story by Dante Gabriel Rossetti, published in the Pre-Raphaelite magazine *The Germ* in 1850. The tale of Chiaro dell' Erma concerns an imaginary Italian painter who in a dream is vouchsafed a vision of a woman with long, loose hair, whom he recognizes as his own soul, or anima:

> It seemed that the first thoughts he had ever known were given to him as at first from her eyes, and he knew her hair to be the golden veil through which he beheld his dreams . . .

The vision bids Chiaro paint her image and the result is a masterpiece.

This high-flown conflation of subject and object need not be taken too solemnly; clearly the young artists hardly required such excuses for painting pictures of pretty women. But it indicates the exalted level at which they aspired to represent womanhood. And it is worth noting that, as a metaphor of artistic creativity, this idea was shared by artists whose own desires were not aroused by lovely women. Simeon Solomon, for instance, was himself homosexually inclined, but his depiction of *The Painter's Pleasaunce* [6] shows the same image of inspiration as *Hand and Soul*. This watercolour in the 'Venetian' mode of the early 1860s shows an artist in period costume painting a beautiful woman and attended by a serving girl bearing refreshments. Flowers and fruits decorate the canvas.

The simple harmony of the composition is interrupted, but not broken, by the diagonal line of the easel, pulling the central figure to the right, to compensate for the fact that his back is towards the serving girl. The formal balance thus achieved contributes to the meaning of the image: the male artist in relation to female model, muse and maidservant — the three main roles allotted to women in the production of pictorial art. In life, of course, the maid was frequently replaced by the wife, who provided or at least organized the necessary domestic services and creature comforts required by the artist. Although historical paintings of painters were popular with nineteenth-century artists as claims to kinship with the genius of the past, *The Painter's Pleasaunce* is remarkable in thus candidly presenting the contemporary relationship between artist and woman.

6 Simeon Solomon, The Painter's Pleasaunce, *1861.*

Edward Burne-Jones, of the second Pre-Raphaelite generation, handled this theme with more sophistication in his various versions of the Pygmalion myth. *Pygmalion and the Image* presents the artist – here a vaguely Renaissance sculptor – producing an image of feminine beauty so perfect that love, in the shape of the goddess Venus, brings the statue to life. In the first frame of the sequence, *The Heart Desires* [7], Pygmalion meditates before a classical statue of the Three Graces, while two young living graces cross a sunlit courtyard. In *The Hand Refrains* [8], the sculptor stands back, tools in hand, awed by the cool loveliness of his creation. With *The Godhead Fires* [9], marble turns to warm pink flesh at Venus's touch, and the figures' arms are linked in a life-giving rhythm. In the final image, *The Soul Attains [10]*, the artist kneels in homage to the living beauty. All is passionate but chaste, in a metaphor of creation: beauty and art combine in the figure of woman. And throughout Burne-Jones's work, 'the image of a beautiful woman was used as a symbol of the artist's mental life and spirit'. [2]

The classical inspiration and treatment of *Pygmalion and the Image*, which dates from the 1870s, raise some of the difficulties of defining Pre-Raphaelite art – a term which did not come into general use until relatively late in the century, when historical and artistic lineages derived from the original Brotherhood were being established. Originally, as the name implies, the Pre-Raphaelites were opposed to High Renaissance and later art, with its neo-classical themes and styles, and admired the direct, unsophisticated imagination of early Italian and Flemish art. However, a broader definition of Pre-Raphaelitism now prevails, which distinguishes phases and styles within the movement and includes a wide range of work showing distinct Pre-Raphaelite influence even where the artist was neither personally associated with the Brotherhood and its disciples nor a formal adherent to its principles.

The movement began in 1848, with the formation of the Pre-Raphaelite Brotherhood (or PRB), and its challenge to academic art evolved over the succeeding half-century alongside other modes of painting. Pictures in the Pre-Raphaelite style were still produced as late as the 1920s, impelled not by pastiche but by a strong although residual impulse from the original source.

Characteristically, although not universally, Pre-Raphaelite art is composed of shallow spaces, flat planes, luminous or cinematic colour with clarity of definition, in thinly applied paint. Its content and meanings are heightened and symbolic rather than anecdotal or simply descriptive, conveying intensity of feeling and significance – which can come gloriously close to comedy when the visual rhetoric topples over into absurdity.

Some of the artists working in the Pre-Raphaelite manner were women, often sisters, wives or daughters of male artists. The relationship of women artists to the standard conventions of masculine creativity and feminine inspiration was naturally different from that of their male colleagues. Yet art comes not only from within but also from the prevailing culture, and, pictorially, the work of women within the Pre-Raphaelite circle tends to deploy similar imagery. In general, this study addresses itself to the art rather than the artist. Women, however, occupied a special place in the artistic world as well as on the easel, and their personal relationship to painting cannot be ignored.

Edward Burne-Jones, Pygmalion and the Image *series, 1878: 7* The Heart Desires; *8* The Hand Refrains; *9* The Godhead Fires; *10* The Soul Attains.

10

Bohemians
and Stunners

In 1848 the young painters who founded the semi-secret society they called the PRB were on the verge of manhood, at the start of their professional careers. There were, originally, seven Pre-Raphaelite Brothers, but only three emerged as major figures in the world of painting – John Everett Millais, William Holman Hunt and Dante Gabriel Rossetti. Of the other Brothers, Thomas Woolner was a sculptor; F. G. Stephens became a respected art critic and chronicler of the movement; William Michael Rossetti, Gabriel's brother, became editor, critic and archivist of the movement; while James Collinson resigned, on religious grounds, even before the dissolution of the group.

Millais, Hunt and Rossetti met as students at the Royal Academy Schools, the main source of art training in London at that time. Their families belonged to the respectable but not wealthy urban middle class, and the young painters were therefore obliged to make their own ways in the world. Fame and fortune were their goals, but their ideals were not materialistic: from their families the painters inherited a high-minded moral sense based on the respectable pieties of middle-class religion, for the theories of evolution had yet to be publicized, and freethinking atheism and agnostic doubt were not yet widespread.

Despite the propriety of their backgrounds, the members of the PRB were no respecters of convention. Their innovative painting style, which startled the art establishment out of its stale, 'sloshy' mode based on tired practice derived from the precepts of the great eighteenth-century founder of the Royal Academy – whom Millais scornfully nicknamed 'Sir Sloshua Reynolds' – was accompanied by firm and idealistic views on artistic conduct.

11 *Dante Gabriel Rossetti,*
Woman in Yellow *(Annie Miller), 1863.*

As Holman Hunt noted, artists were 'a class of men . . . excused for some licentiousness' where female models were concerned. Some Academicians were renowned for their enjoyment of fleshly pleasures, both on the canvas and on the couch. By contrast, the young Pre-Raphaelite Brothers and their associates – for a larger group of friends and fellow painters always attached itself to the inner circle – were conscious of a duty to behave honourably and respectfully towards women. Indeed, a large element of their artistic inspiration came from this very desire to elevate and idealize women, which they sought to express also in personal behaviour.

At the same time, they rejected humbug and hypocrisy. With their high spirits and high aspirations, they challenged Victorian notions of 'correctness' based purely on convention. And as the century progressed, they became identified with the unconventional and easy-going bohemian lifestyle increasingly ascribed to artists in the nineteenth century, following Henri Murger's depiction of the Parisian scene in *Vie de Bohème*.

Among the other artists associated with the Brotherhood and Pre-Raphaelitism were Ford Madox Brown, slightly older than the PRB; Arthur Hughes, who shared Millais's studio in the early years; the Scottish-born sculptor Alexander Munro; and Walter Deverell, a fellow student at the Royal Academy Schools, who died tragically young. Towards the end of the 1850s, new recruits emerged, prominent among whom were Edward Burne-Jones, William Morris, Simeon Solomon and Val Prinsep.

However, this is not the place for a detailed account of all the artists associated with Pre-Raphaelitism, the history of which is, some might say, exhaustively documented elsewhere. Readers wishing to know more about individual painters or the chronology of the movement are referred to the many excellent accounts, both scholarly and popular, listed in the Select Bibliography (see p. 158). It should be noted, though, that the artists now known collectively as 'the Pre-Raphaelites' did not form a completely homogeneous group. Indeed, Millais, a founder member, soon joined the despised Royal Academy and from at least 1860 more or less abandoned his Pre-Raphaelite principles in favour of quicker, easier and more lucrative society portraits and sentimental scenes. Holman Hunt remained faithful to the original pictorial and pious impulses, but ceased to meet socially with his former colleagues, believing that Rossetti's moral behaviour had lapsed; this and his travels to Palestine took Hunt away from what may be termed the later mainstream of Pre-Raphaelitism.

In the early years, however, the painters were united by their youth, their idealism, and their search for models. It is a myth that the Brothers cruised the streets of London picking up pretty girls; they were in fact too frightened to do this lest they should inadvertently accost prostitutes, whom they had been taught to abhor. And any respectable girl would certainly refuse such advances, since it was still considered a social offence to speak to someone who had not been formally introduced. So models were sought chiefly among family and friends, or in the private sketching clubs that flourished in central London, providing drawing practice and professional gossip.

12 John Everett Millais, Miss Anne
Ryan, *c. 1853.*

Anne Ryan, one of Millais's favourite models, first appeared at an evening
sketching club early in 1852. She was 'a little beauty', noted the painter George
Boyce, who had an eye for a pretty girl. Anne posed for Millais as several

heroines – as the Catholic girl in *A Huguenot on St Bartholomew's Day* (1851–2), with her dark hair painted blonde, and as the Puritan girl in *The Proscribed Royalist, 1651* (1852–3).

It is thought that Anne Ryan was of Irish descent – the famine of the 'hungry forties' in Ireland led many families to seek work in England – a working-class girl turning her pretty face and figure to practical account by working as a professional model. Millais was evidently fond of her, and probably painted the small portrait now in the Tate Gallery as a gift, perhaps to mark her wedding [12]. But her fate was unhappy, if obscure. 'Alas for Miss Ryan', wrote Millais's son, 'her beauty proved a fatal gift: she married an ostler and her later history is a sad one. My father was always reluctant to speak of it, feeling perhaps that the publicity he had given to her beauty might in some small measure have helped (as the saying is) to turn her head.' [1]

Something similar seems to have happened to Ellen Frazer, whom Rossetti spotted working as a maidservant in the house of the sculptor Alexander Munro, and who may have been brought from Inverness, the Munros' home town. Rossetti drew her demure, sweet face in the early years of the Brotherhood [14]; in another soft pencil drawing she can be seen wearing her servant's cap and apron, with her sleeves turned back to the elbow ready for work. According to family tradition, Ellen Frazer's head was also 'turned' by this interest in her as a model, 'and she had to be dismissed'. [2]

Elizabeth Siddall's entry into the Pre-Raphaelite circle as a model was more successful. First seen by Walter Deverell working in a bonnet shop, she was asked to sit for the figure of Viola in his *Twelfth Night* (1850). After this she went to work for Holman Hunt, posing as a British girl in his *A Converted British Family Sheltering a Christian Missionary from the Persecution of the Druids* (1850), then for Millais, and finally for Rossetti.

Rossetti fell in love with the pale, red-haired milliner and transformed her life by encouraging her own pursuit of art. 'A result all but inevitable ensued', wrote Rossetti's first biographer, 'when to the attractions of youth and beauty is added the magnetism that springs from kindred tastes and occupations. The close intimacy in the relationship of master and pupil gave every opportunity for successful wooing, and Miss Siddall became affianced to her teacher.' [3]

Launched on an artistic career of her own, Lizzie, as she was known, changed the spelling of her surname to 'Siddal' and abandoned professional modelling. Thereafter, she is seen in numerous portraits, sketches and drawings, among the finest work Rossetti produced: sitting, reading, sewing, resting and at her easel

14 *Dante Gabriel Rossetti*, Ellen Frazer, c. 1852.

13 *Dante Gabriel Rossetti*, A Lady Seated at an Easel *(Elizabeth Siddal)*, c. 1854.

and drawing-board [13]. His images are tender and loving; her own self-portrait in oils [15] suggests a more anxious and self-critical young woman than Rossetti's beautiful but decidedly glamorous portrayals [16].

Rossetti was, of course, painting Lizzie as a 'stunner', the slang term for a good-looking woman. Holman Hunt had discovered one too: her name was Annie Miller, and she had grown up in a slum yard behind his studio in Chelsea. He saw the squalor in which she lived – her luxuriant hair infested with lice – and determined to rescue her. First, Annie was employed as a model; she was then sent to learn her lessons and her manners – how to speak, dress and behave in polite company. When, in 1854, Holman Hunt left for the Middle East, he placed Annie in the care of the PRB, as an occasional model. She grew into a handsome woman and was later renowned for her refinement [11, 17].

15 Elizabeth Siddal, Self Portrait, *1853–4.*

16 Dante Gabriel Rossetti, Portrait of Elizabeth Siddal, *1854.*

Millais was the first of the Brothers to marry, rescuing his bride Effie Gray from a loveless, sexless marriage to John Ruskin, art critic and friend and patron of the Pre-Raphaelites. On holiday in Scotland with her husband and Millais, Effie confided her troubles to the young painter. The following year she left Ruskin and obtained a legal annulment; quietly, after a decent interval, she and Millais were married.

Effie modelled for Millais both before and after their marriage, but her role in the Pre-Raphaelite story was short, as domestic and maternal duties increasingly claimed her time.

Under Ruskin's patronage, Elizabeth Siddal spent the winter of 1855–6 in the south of France for the sake of her health. In London, Rossetti's artistic inspiration was fired by a new type of stunner – bold, blonde and independent. Her name was Louisa Ruth Herbert, and she was an actress – not an occupation for a 'respectable' woman [18]. 'Did you ever see her? O my eye!' wrote Rossetti excitedly. 'She has the most varied and highest expression I ever saw in a woman's face, besides abundant beauty, golden hair, etc.' [4] One of Rossetti's pencil portraits of Ruth Herbert, of 1859, includes a pointing finger and the word 'stunner'. And in one watercolour portrait a gold ivy-leaved frame acts as a glorious foil to her resplendent head.

17 Dante Gabriel Rossetti, Annie Miller, c. *1860.*

In 1858, Rossetti met another blonde stunner, who used the name Fanny Cornforth and first accosted him while soliciting in the street. Fanny seems to have preferred modelling to prostitution, and was soon sitting to several painters including Rossetti (whose mistress she became), Edward Burne-Jones, George Boyce (who also employed Annie Miller) and J. R. Spencer Stanhope.

Fanny was a fine-looking woman, who sat for many of Rossetti's 'visions of carnal loveliness': the sexy three-quarter-length female figures that during the 1860s increasingly displaced the earlier religious and literary subjects in his work, as the aesthetics of form and colour gained ground at the expense of narrative and composition. 'I am now painting a lady plaiting her hair', he wrote to a client in 1863, while busy with Fanny as *Fazio's Mistress* (sometimes also called *Aurelia*) [19]. 'This is in oil and chiefly a piece of colour.' [5] Ten years later, when Fanny had grown fat and Rossetti, punning affectionately from 'Fan', called her 'dear Elephant', he described the picture as 'the one where you are seated doing your hair before a glass . . . It is exactly like the funny old elephant, as like as I ever did.' [6] The title, *Fazio's Mistress*, was taken from a poem by Fazio degli Uberti included in Rossetti's recently published translations of Italian poetry, *Early Italian Poets* (1861).

Loose, luxuriant hair was an emblem of female sexuality in Pre-Raphaelite painting, just as it is today the chief signifier of the term 'Pre-Raphaelite'. And in *Fazio's Mistress* we may well have a clue to the rippling effect of so much Pre-Raphaelite hair. After washing, the tresses were plaited while still wet – as Fanny is shown doing – and then allowed to dry, creating a naturally crimped look.

The women who posed for the Pre-Raphaelites' paintings are often described as passive, silent, sometimes bewildered beauties, discovered by the artists and delivered on canvas to a marvelling world. But, like the careers of some twentieth-century film stars, this story probably conceals a good deal of active intelligence and ambition. Most of the celebrated Pre-Raphaelite models came from lower- or working-class backgrounds; like the painters, they had to use their gifts and talents to the best advantage.

Many, if not most, of the artists seem actively to have sought out working-class women as models and prospective brides – not only Rossetti and Holman Hunt, but also Ford Madox Brown, who married his young model Emma Hill; Frederick Stephens, an original PRB member whose young wife Clara was barely literate; Frederick Sandys, who had a long liaison with a gypsy woman and later eloped with seventeen-year-old Mary Jones; and also William Morris, who married a stablehand's daughter, Jane Burden, and took her to live in a 'Palace of Art'. Frederic Shields took his young model Matilda to the altar the moment she reached marriageable age, perhaps to save her as much as himself from temptation; the marriage was not a success.

Failing to persuade Annie Miller of the benefits he could offer as a husband, Holman Hunt went in search of a middle-class bride. Rejected by the lovely Julia Jackson [24], niece of Pre-Raphaelite photographer Julia Margaret Cameron, he eventually married Fanny Waugh, daughter of a wealthy pharmacist. She died tragically in childbirth, and ten years later Hunt married her sister Edith; the ceremony took place abroad as marriage to a deceased wife's sister was still illegal in Britain at this date.

Edith Waugh had in fact worked and waited carefully to land her catch. And comparable aspirations may be attributed to other women in the Pre-Raphaelite circle. Marriage was, after all, one of the few routes to upward mobility and security open to women with looks and intelligence in the Victorian age.

Some attempts to rise in the world through association with these artists were unsuccessful: in addition to the unlucky Anne Ryan and Ellen Frazer, of whom so little is known, there was a laundress named Ellen Smith, discovered in Chelsea by Rossetti. She sat for 'several of his sweetest pictures', recorded George Boyce, 'until the poor girl got her face sadly cut about and disfigured by a brute of a soldier, and then of course she was of no more use as a model.' [7] Another of Rossetti's longstanding models was a quiet, respectable dressmaker named Alice Wilding, whose intelligence scarcely matched her striking looks. She called herself Alexa and, to general disbelief, dreamt of a stage career.

By no means all of the renowned Pre-Raphaelite models were recognized as beautiful in their time. Some, like Lizzie Siddal and Jane Burden, would have been generally regarded as tall, ungainly and plain, at a time when petite, delicate prettiness was admired. Lizzie had a prominent upper lip and top teeth, Jane's complexion was pallid, and her eyebrows thick and dark.

18 Dante Gabriel Rossetti, Ruth Herbert, c. *1858–9.*

19 Dante Gabriel Rossetti, Fazio's Mistress, *1863.*

It is thus one of the remarkable achievements of the Pre-Raphaelite painters that they were able to alter and enlarge Victorian definitions of beauty, and create a 'look' that has remained popular with painters and public for so long. The chief credit for this must go to Rossetti, the leader of the movement in so many ways, and also to Jane Morris, known as Janey, the favourite model of his later years, immortalized as the dark, long-throated, limber-fingered woman who gazes soulfully from so many photographs and canvases [3, 20, 21].

Loyally, Edward Burne-Jones called his fiancée Georgiana Macdonald 'my stunner'. However, she had few illusions about her appearance, being small in stature, with a flat profile, thin lips and meagre, mousy hair. Nevertheless, she featured in many of her husband's early works, and his later portrait of her as steadfast wife and mother is a true, if idealized, image [22]. Beauty, after all, *is* in the eye of the beholder — and the artist. Certainly, Burne-Jones believed that portraits should aim at conveying the essential soul, not the accidents of nature and superficial appearance.

Unhappily for Georgie, Burne-Jones was also beguiled by another form of beauty in the shape of Maria Zambaco, with whom he pursued a tempestuous affair; her features are repeatedly visible in his work of the later 1860s and 1870s [1]. Maria belonged to the Greek community in London, which provided new models for the painters: well-to-do, artistic and independent women. Together, the cousins Maria Zambaco, Aglaia Coronio and Marie Spartali were known as the Three Graces [23].

Even more interestingly, perhaps, this group demonstrates another important facet of the women depicted in Pre-Raphaelite paintings: many of them were active artists in their own right. Maria Zambaco was a sculptor and medallist, while Marie Spartali, who married American journalist W. J. Stillman, became a painter, like Elizabeth Siddal. Jane Morris was a well-known embroiderer, with a renowned eye for colour and design. Anna Mary Howitt and Julia Margaret Cameron have already been mentioned as artists; to their names should be added those of Joanna Mary Boyce, who married painter Henry Wells; Emily Hunt, Holman's sister; Rebecca Solomon, sister to two painters; and Emma Sandys. All of these were painters in their own right.

The later phase of Pre-Raphaelitism also highlights several women painters — Lucy and Catherine Madox Brown, trained in their father's studio, Eleanor Fortescue-Brickdale, Evelyn de Morgan and Kate Bunce. Their work is relatively unfamiliar and inaccessible, although now growing in popularity.

As artists, the women were less clearly successful than the male Pre-Raphaelite painters. As images, however, they dominate the scene. There are in fact three main types of Pre-Raphaelite 'stunner', which correspond in part to the phases of Pre-Raphaelite art and in part to the ideas of feminity current in the Victorian age. The first and earliest type is the fair, demure, modest maiden with her innocent attractions [24]; the second is the proud golden beauty who might

20 John R. Parsons, photograph of Jane Morris, *1865.*

21 Dante Gabriel Rossetti, Pandora, *1869.*

borrow a term from later 'sex goddesses'; and the third is the dark, enigmatic siren or *femme fatale,* who represented the *fin de siècle* idea of the Eternal Feminine.

These images naturally corresponded to the different physical appearances of the various women who were Pre-Raphaelite models. But while looking at the images of feminine allurement and their variants displayed in the following pages, it is important to recognize that art and actuality seldom coincide completely, although they may become confused. The metaphors and fantasies of art are not to be identified as the behaviour and feelings of real life, especially where the Pre-Raphaelite women were concerned. The personalities and conduct of the women who sat for the pictures – which are not portraits – cannot be inferred from their images. As individuals, they often inspired and contributed to the artistic process, but the paintings are representations not of individual women but of imaginative ideas – images of the Pre-Raphaelite Woman in all her guises.

22 Edward Burne-Jones, Georgiana Burne-Jones with Children, *1883.*

23 Dante Gabriel Rossetti, Maria Zambaco, *1870.*

24 *Valentine (Val) Cameron Prinsep,* Head of a Girl *(possibly Julia Jackson), ?1875.*

Holy Virgins

The piety of the age and of their families made the young painters of the PRB naturally attracted to religious subjects. At least at the outset of their careers they believed in the moral purpose of art, as did their early patrons, such as John Ruskin and his father, or Thomas Combe of Oxford. Together with their natural human interest in the impulses of youth, this early Victorian piety drew the painters towards the portrayal of saintly young females, either the Virgin Mary, mother of Christ and archetype of sanctified womanhood, or girls renouncing the world and the flesh for the purposes of religious devotion. The saint and the nun were the resulting motifs.

The saints of the Catholic Church were unfamiliar in Victorian Protestant Britain, where Catholic emancipation was a recent event, and were rediscovered by the painters in the Christian iconography of early Renaissance art from Italy and northern Europe, the main pictorial influences on the Pre-Raphaelites. Moreover, the Anglo-Catholic tendencies in the Church of England, together with the conversion to Rome of several important figures such as Cardinal Newman, also helped to legitimize the artistic representation of saints. Nevertheless, the movement was sometimes attacked as papistical for its treatment of religious themes.

'That picture of mine was a symbol of female excellence,' Rossetti explained of his first major work, *The Girlhood of Mary Virgin* (1849) [25], 'the Virgin being taken as its highest type.' [1] It has, also, a personal meaning, in reference to the devout upbringing provided by the artist's mother, Frances Rossetti, who sat for the figure of St Anne, Mary's mother. His younger sister Christina sat for the Virgin, 'her appearance being excellently adapted to my purpose', as Rossetti wrote to his godfather. [2]

25 *Dante Gabriel Rossetti,* The Girlhood of Mary Virgin, *1849.*

The Virgin is shown under St Anne's instruction meekly embroidering onto a red stole a lily, symbol of her own purity, while her medieval-style books are inscribed with the names of the cardinal virtues – charity, faith, hope, fortitude – apt emblems of womanhood. The archaic, sacred quality of the image is reinforced by other symbolic details, including St Joseph pruning a vine to represent the coming of Christ, the seven-thorned briar on the floor, and the touches of gold paint in the haloes and the Virgin's hair. 'The picture smacks of Mariolatry', commented a recent critic, [3] and was indeed so interpreted when it appeared. It is only saved from undue religiosity by the Virgin's solemn, slightly anxious expression: she seems aware of the weight of symbolism surrounding her, and of her own inadequacy to the task.

Mary's embroidered stole – an ecclesiastical anachronism indicating that the picture is not a historical representation of life in ancient Palestine but a portrayal of the religious significance of the Blessed Virgin – reappears in Rossetti's next major work, on the traditional theme of the Annunciation, *Ecce Ancilla Domini* (1850) [27] – 'Behold the handmaid of the Lord', Mary's response to the Angel's announcement that she was favoured by God.

This is a strange picture, tall and narrow and very pale. It has been described as unique in nineteenth-century painting, foreshadowing the much later work of the early abstract artists, and it displays in extreme form the startling, original qualities associated with the initial Pre-Raphaelite impulse.

At the moment the archangel Gabriel appears to her (a scene depicted in countless religious works of art) this Virgin is 'in bed, but without any bedclothes on, an arrangement which may be justified in consideration of the hot climate', according to the rather apologetic words of the artist's brother, writing in the PRB *Journal* in 1849, as if countering allegations of indecency. The Virgin's figure is in fact fully covered by her shapeless nightgown, but there is nevertheless a disturbing tension in the composition which hints at something indelicate. This is partly achieved through the narrow shape of the canvas, and through the way Mary shrinks back against the wall in maiden modesty, as if trying to evade the violation of the archangel's lily stem, which points directly at her womb, on the end of which her gaze is locked. The symbolic message – the divine conception of Christ – is clear. The intense feeling may owe something also to submerged sexual references; the Lord's handmaid was chosen to bear his Son for her spotless maidenhood and spiritual perfection: feminine ideals which were also sought, at a less elevated level, in Victorian wives.

Once again, Christina Rossetti sat for the Virgin (although preliminary studies were also made from a nude professional model), expressing the devout demeanour also visible in her early portrait by PRB member James Collinson, to whom she was engaged while the painting was in progress [26]. In 1850 Collinson resigned from the Brotherhood and rejoined the Catholic Church; at the same time he renounced his engagement, to Christina's great relief. As a

27 (opposite) Dante Gabriel Rossetti, Ecce Ancilla Domini, 1850.

26 James Collinson, Christina Rossetti, c. 1850.

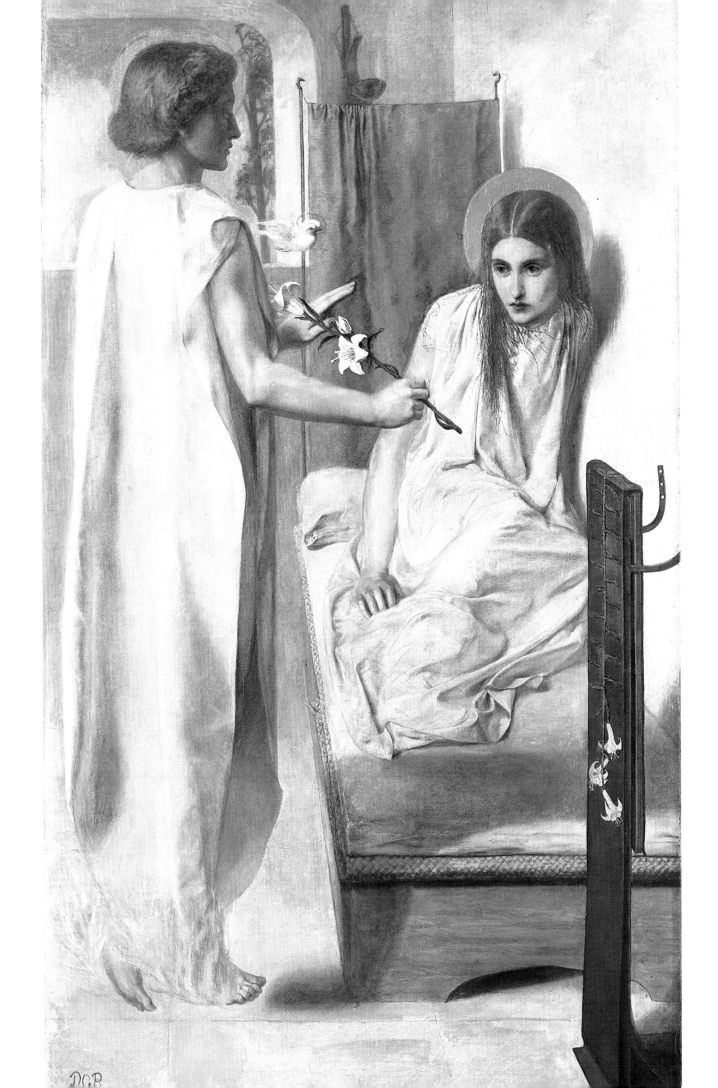

28 *William Holman Hunt,* Claudio and Isabella, *1850.*

young woman she possessed a fierce wit and strong emotions, visible in her writings; with her lively interest in the Brotherhood and her own poetic contributions to *The Germ,* she may almost be counted an honorary Pre-Raphaelite Sister. Certainly she rhymed wittily on its members and followed its progress and dissolution.

The link between virgin purity and violation was more explicit in Holman Hunt's *Claudio and Isabella* [28], begun in the same year as *Ecce Ancilla Domini.* The subject is taken from the moral conflict in Shakespeare's *Measure for Measure,* between Claudio, a young nobleman condemned to death, and his sister the religious Isabella. Claudio asks Isabella to sacrifice her virginity to the cruel Angelo in order to save his own life.

Walter Deverell modelled for the figure of Claudio, whose moral state is indicated by his velvet and fur-trimmed garments and of course by the shackle on his leg to symbolize the sinfulness that holds him captive. Isabella, by contrast, is dressed in a simple white habit, probably from the Order of St Clare; she stands bathed in light, her hands placed compassionately on her brother's heart. Behind her, the sunshine, apple blossom and distant church spire all emphasize her state of spiritual grace. The artist's moral judgement is thus represented in light and shade.

The same nun's habit was used in 1851 by Charles Collins in his picture *Convent Thoughts* [29], which depicts a young novice or postulant in a cloistered garden meditating on a passion-flower, symbol of the Crucifixion. This has the appearance of a devotional work, the canvas being set in an arched frame with a Latin inscription taken from *The Song of Solomon* – 'As the lily . . .'. Charles Collins was a minor member of the Pre-Raphaelite circle, a close friend of Millais and unsuccessful suitor of Christina's devout sister Maria Rossetti. According to Millais and Hunt, Collins's original inspiration had been Shelley's 'The Sensitive Plant', and like Anna Howitt's picture would simply have shown a young woman tending a flower garden. But, 'being disappointed in an affair of the heart' – this may refer to Maria's rejection – Collins altered his conception to that of a contemplative nun.[4]

This novice is clearly a maiden. The model was 'a very beautiful young lady' named Frances Ludlow, known to Collins's family. The nun's spiritual state is represented symbolically by the flowers; tall Madonna lilies reach out towards her, water-lilies pick up the theme, and roses contrast with the thornless Virgin, who is seen in the illuminated manuscript held by the figure showing 'a crucifixion and an annunciation, allusions to the Holy Spouse to whom she is betrothed as well as to the role of wife and mother she has spurned.'[5] Purity is all-pervasive: even the goldfish turn chastely pale as they swim in the reflection

29 *Charles Collins,* Convent Thoughts, *1851.*

SICVT LILIAM

of her habit. There is, however, some sense of conflict between the cool, sexless seclusion of the convent setting and the profusion of blossoms. Elsewhere in Victorian thought pretty young girls like this were destined for plucking, and *Convent Thoughts* may contain a suppressed reference to Maria Rossetti's strict piety and the rejection of her suitor. Later, her religious devotion led her to enter an Anglican Sisterhood.

The revival of these convent-like religious orders 'brought together three important strands in Victorian life: the need to respond to poverty and social distress, the widespread religious renaissance . . . and the problem of redundant women.' [6] The first full censuses in mid-century revealed a striking imbalance in the numbers of males and females in the British population and there was consequent anxiety over who would provide for those women who could never marry.

The first Anglican Order for women was founded in 1845 in London, close to the church where the Rossetti women worshipped, and where the Sisters of Mercy attended services dressed in their distinctive habits. The Sisterhoods aroused much contemporary controversy: on the one hand they were examples of religious faith, self-denial and devotion; on the other they suggested 'popery' at a time of continuing anti-Catholic suspicion and, more worryingly, female independence. Sometimes regarded as useful alternatives for the thousands of supposedly 'surplus' women, convents were at the same time distrusted for giving women limited but real freedom, through their vows of obedience, outside the patriarchal jurisdiction of the family.

30 *Dante Gabriel Rossetti,* St Elizabeth of Hungary Kneeling with her Companions, *c. 1852.*

Similar arguments were at issue in Charles Kingsley's play *The Saint's Tragedy*, published in 1848, which presented the life of 'St Elizabeth of Hungary, Landgravine of Thuringia, Saint of the Romish Calendar'. To Kingsley, Elizabeth's renunciation of her crown and worldly goods demonstrated a wilful neglect of wifely and social duties, which ought to rank above those of religion. To the young Pre-Raphaelites, however, she was something of a saintly heroine. Between 1848 and 1850 James Collinson produced a large painting, *The Renunciation of Queen Elizabeth of Hungary* (1848–50) [31] showing the saint in church at the foot of an image of Christ, with her coronet beside her on the floor and worried ladies and courtiers all around. Shortly after this was painted, the artist rejoined the Catholic Church and renounced his engagement to Christina; 'he must have felt the portrayal of the renunciation of human love . . . as strongly applicable to his own problems.' [7]

An early drawing by Millais shows *St Elizabeth Washing the Feet of Pilgrims* (c. 1848) with her beatification sketched in on the background wall. Charles Collins contributed to the series with *The Devout Childhood of St Elizabeth of Hungary* (1852), and an unfinished sketch by Rossetti of three kneeling figures, probably all drawn from Elizabeth Siddal during her professional modelling days, has been identified as *St Elizabeth of Hungary Kneeling with her Companions* (c. 1852) [30]. All have close textual links to scenes from Kingsley's play.

31 James Collinson, The Renunciation of Queen Elizabeth of Hungary, *1848–50.*

The holy virgin in her convent was the theme of Tennyson's short poem 'St Agnes' Eve', quoted earlier. Despite the pious subject, ardent feeling overtakes the verse as the novice, contemplating her approaching vows, imagines her union with Christ:

> A light upon the shining sea –
> The Bridegroom with his bride!

In 1854, Millais produced a detailed ink drawing of *St Agnes' Eve*, showing the nun looking out on a snowy convent garden. Snowdrops, the flower of St Agnes, decorate both her habit and the leaded window she faces. The composition was based on a portrait Millais had planned of Effie while she was still married to Ruskin; this was abandoned when the mutual attraction of artist and sitter became acknowledged. The union at first seemed impossible – divorce was virtually unknown at this date – and the small *St Agnes' Eve* picture has been interpreted as 'an image of the artist's own yearning, which was at the time apparently hopeless, for his future wife – and equally of hers for him'. [8] Millais gave the drawing to Effie, who recognized its message, discerning Millais's features in the nun's profile; Ruskin also guessed at its significance, making 'veiled accusations' about the artist to his wife.

According to Effie, the idea of painting a full-sized picture 'with nuns in it' first occurred to Millais during their honeymoon in 1855. *The Vale of Rest* [32] was begun in the garden of Effie's family home in Perth in 1858 and incorporated elements of an old graveyard nearby. It is a curious and disturbing intimation of mortality.

The young nuns are good-looking wenches, attractively attired. Yet one is digging a grave, perhaps her own, in which she stands. The other sits, with a skull attached to her rosary, while two yellow wreaths reflect the sunset, and a coffin-shaped cloud, an omen of death, hovers in the sky. All is indicative of old age and the end of life, a message that conflicts with the girls' health and vigour. The spectator's uneasiness is compounded by the seated nun's direct gaze, as if she is aware of our presence. Yet how should anyone else, especially a stranger, be within that dark enclosing convent wall? Or perhaps the nuns' immurement is meant to be read as death itself; they are 'lost' to the everyday world, or more particularly to the men they might have wed. Whatever its import, this is a strange theme to have been conceived during a honeymoon.

In the later years of Pre-Raphaelitism, the representation of nuns and holy virgins tended to disappear, although images, often prurient and offensive in their depiction of lovely girls captive within convent walls, continued to appear at the annual Royal Academy exhibitions. 'The projection of romantic and latent erotic appeal into the depiction of religious maidens generated what might be termed the "rescued nun syndrome",' according to a recent scholar, [9] in which handsome lovers succeed in plucking their sweethearts from the living burial of the conventual life.

32 (previous page) John Everett Millais, The Vale of Rest, 1858.

In 1874 Maria Rossetti formally joined the Sisters of Mercy religious Order, becoming 'one of those old things you see going about in a sort of coal-scuttle and umbrella costume', as her brother unkindly wrote to his earthy mistress Fanny Cornforth.[10] Fanny, incidentally, was one of those 'unfortunates' or fallen women whom Maria's Order aimed to reclaim from sin. Maria's sister-in-law, the painter Lucy Madox Brown, whose marriage to William Rossetti had helped precipitate the decision, celebrated Maria's vows with a portrait of her in a nun's coif.

33 Eleanor Fortescue-Brickdale,
Guenevere, *1911.*

The decline of the early religious ardour in Pre-Raphaelite art, which had produced intense but sometimes awkward images, made way, by the 1870s, for smoother emotion and execution. Comparison of Burne-Jones's *Annunciation* (1879) [35] with Rossetti's *Ecce Ancilla Domini* of thirty years before — with which it shares a tall narrow shape and a composition based on two vertical figures — illustrates the changes in style and feeling, from the intensely religious and iconoclastic to the decorative and mellifluous. Rossetti's archangel, although carried on flames of fire, is a real incarnate vision, while Burne-Jones's messenger hovers halfway up a tree, wings sprouting from androgynous shoulders. The Virgin, robed in perfect draperies, seems hardly startled by the apparition, from which she is in any case safely separated by a long receding corridor. There is little religious feeling in Burne-Jones's picture. It is as if Mary's dramatic moment, so often rehearsed in art, has become simply another aesthetic scene. The face of the Virgin, incidentally, was painted from Julia Jackson. 'Her beauty made people think of Greek goddesses and Elgin marbles', according to a recent writer, with unwitting allusion to the cool perfection of the *Annunciation*; 'her character made them think of madonnas and saints.' [11]

34 *Unidentified photographer,* Girl and Lily, *c. 1910.*

Later images of saints and nuns included J. W. Waterhouse's *The Missal* (1902), with its apparently deliberate echoes of Millais's first *St Agnes' Eve*, and Eleanor Fortescue-Brickdale's unusual image of *Guenevere* (1911) [33]. The latter illustrates Arthur's adulterous queen from Tennyson's *Idylls of the King*, in which she flees from the court to seek sanctuary at Almesbury convent. The poem's force is concentrated in the king's denunciation of the queen's 'polluted flesh'; the painter chooses to represent her penitence and humility. 'Oh shut me round with narrowing nunnery walls, meek maidens!' she implores the sisters:

> So let me . . .
> Pray and be pray'd for; lie before your shrines;
> Do each low office of your holy house:
> Walk your dim cloister, and distribute dole
> To poor sick people . . .

The loaves in Guenevere's basket are evidently destined for such charity.

Devout and sacred figures, usually engaged in prayer, feature with some frequency in Pre-Raphaelite photography. And a final, intriguing image in this sequence of holy femininity is seen in a picture by an unknown photographer, showing a young woman with loose hair and a meditative expression, dressed in archaic, vaguely conventual costume, and holding a large Madonna lily [34]. The figure is surrounded by flowers and foliage and although it is clear that the subject was posed, rather inexpertly, in a conservatory or enclosed yard — one of the pot plants has a visible botanical label — both the theme and the composition, with its single figure and shallow space, suggest direct inspiration from Pre-Raphaelite painting. The image recalls *Convent Thoughts*, while the girl's steady gaze at the lily stem suggests pictorial quotation from *The Girlhood of Mary Virgin* and *Ecce Ancilla Domini* — echoes strong enough to influence this amateur photographer half a century later.

35 *Edward Burne-Jones*, Annunciation,
1879.

Nubile Maidens

The original meaning of 'nubile' was simply 'marriageable', with overtones of budding sexuality. Such maidenly figures, often demurely waiting for husbands but also hinting at awakening desire, are a recurrent theme in Pre-Raphaelite art.

In the early years of the movement, romantic love was still a relatively recent invention. Older notions of marriage based on economic compatibility and parental sanction had given way to the new concept, born of Romanticism, of love as an overwhelming passion that transformed lovers and gave them strength to overcome all obstacles. Indeed, romantic love often thrived on opposition, triumphing – at least in art – over family refusal, poverty, separation, and even death: everlastingly devoted lovers could dream of reunion in or beyond the grave.

More prosaically, romantic love assisted the expansion of industry and Empire, giving ambitious young men the faithful support of young women who would wait patiently or follow their beloveds to the end of the earth. It also provided consolation for the death of loved ones, given the still high mortality rates of the nineteenth century.

In Victorian art and literature the power of romantic love is probably the single most frequent theme, reflected in the rising popularity not only of fiction, with its vast supply of love stories ending in marriage, but also in the rediscovery of legendary lovers such as Romeo and Juliet, Dante and Beatrice, Paolo and Francesca, Lancelot and Guinevere, Tristram and Isolde: themes constantly reworked in painting, poetry and music. A complete account even of Pre-Raphaelite representations of romantic love in this mode would itself fill an entire book: here there is room only for a small selection, and reference in the text to many more pictures than can be illustrated.

36 *Dante Gabriel Rossetti,* Girl at a Lattice, *1862.*

The personal popularity of such pictorial themes among the young PRB is not surprising, since all were youthfully aware of the attractions of the opposite sex, and also conscious of their own lack of income, which in middle-class circles meant deferred matrimony. At the age of most intense romantic feeling, most young men were, in fact, inhibited from proposing to the beloved of their dreams; the results were images of desire and yearning, as in Rossetti's *Girl at a Lattice* (1862) [36]. Moreover, they were all admiring readers of Keats, the poet of true love and pure, passionate romance triumphing over obstacles, as we have seen, in 'The Eve of St Agnes'. Following the publication of Keats's collected works in 1848, this poem provided a chief source of inspiration. In the same year, before the formation of the Brotherhood, Holman Hunt chose to paint the final scene, showing *The Flight of Madeline and Porphyro* (1848), where the lovers steal away past drunken revellers and comatose guards; in the language of flowers a bunch of mistletoe denoted difficulties overcome.

Eight years later Arthur Hughes, himself newly married, produced a three-part pictorial narrative of *The Eve of St Agnes* (1856), which shows Porphyro's approach to the ancient hall, his awakening of Madeline in her chamber, and finally the lovers escaping to their future.

In 1862 Millais tackled the same subject, choosing the erotic climax of the action, as Madeline disrobes in her chamber unaware of Porphyro's watching presence: an apt theme for a painting viewed by the unseen spectator. This *Eve of St Agnes* (1862–3) was painted at night, in the King's Bedroom of the Tudor mansion Knole. Effie posed in the moonlight for the authentic effect, although the figure was later repainted from a professional model, and the final image has little of the urgency of Keats's poem – partly because it is so realistically dark (Millais complained that moonlight was not strong enough to make jewelled colours and fabrics glow, as the verse claimed) and partly because the figure of Madeline is placed at a distance from the spectator, so that little of the throbbing sensuousness of Keats's moment is conveyed.

In some respects the most erotic image inspired by the poem comes from the academic painter Daniel Maclise, who in 1868 showed his *Madeline after Prayer* at the Royal Academy. This, incidentally, demonstrates the growing influence of Pre-Raphaelitism, such that by the 1860s the poetic impulse associated with the movement was widespread and no longer confined to a small group. At the same time, Maclise's image lacks Pre-Raphaelite sensitivity: his Madeline is partly a pin-up, with her snowy bosom half-exposed as she loosens the jewels from her hair.

The Brotherhood also drew inspiration from other poems by Keats. Among their earliest proposals was a projected sequence of illustrations to 'Isabella, or the Pot of Basil', the classic Romantic tale of young tragedy in which Lorenzo's love for Isabella is opposed by her brothers, who conspire to murder him. In a macabre celebration of eternal devotion, Isabella rescues Lorenzo's body and cuts off his beloved head:

Love never dies, but lives, immortal Lord . . .
Pale Isabella kiss'd it, and low moan'd
'Twas love; cold – dead indeed, but not dethroned.

She keeps the head in an urn, planted with basil and watered with her tears, until discovered by her brothers. Then she pines away to death, the very personification of constancy and romance.

In the projected sequence, Holman Hunt chose to show *Lorenzo at his Desk in the Warehouse* [37], working for the proud brothers, aware of his beloved's quiet entry:

He knew whose gentle hand was on the latch
Before the door had given her to his eyes.

The composition 'comments on Victorian attitudes to courtship and marriage', [1] and on the class consciousness that hindered many matches. Isabella is a demure, middle-class maiden, set against a background of exploited workers – 1848 was of course the year of revolution in Europe and Chartism in Britain – which relates both to the artist's personal experience as a warehouse clerk in London and to the poem's theme of love overcoming obstacles. The lovers in the drawing are visually and symbolically separated by the vertical line of the door and an unfriendly-looking dog.

37 William Holman Hunt, Lorenzo at his Desk in the Warehouse, *1858–60.*

The same hounds feature in Millais's painting *Isabella* [38] showing the lovers at table unable to conceal their emotion:

> They could not in the self-same mansion dwell
> Without some stir of heat, some malady;
> They could not sit at meals but feel how well
> It soothed each to be the other by . . .

If isolated from the rest of the group, Isabella and Lorenzo personify idealistic romance, expressed in his intense gaze and in her shy face and gentle touch on the greyhound's docile head. As the true lovers exchange hearts, they share a blood orange. Hints of the tragedy to come are given in the painting's many narrative details – a beheading scene on the plate, and the 'ominous garden pots' on the balcony. Note also the carved bench end with the cryptic 'PRB' initials. William Rossetti, incidentally, was the model for the young Lorenzo, Fred Stephens for the brother in the black hat, and Walter Deverell for the man beside him. Mary Hodgkinson, Millais's married sister-in-law, sat for Isabella; an ink study drawn with the artist's delicate precision shows a sweet but vacant profile, which does not quite convey the courage and determination later displayed by Keats's heroine.

Yet *Isabella* is not a simple image of young love. It is charged with a disruptive sexual force in the phallic thrust of the brother's leg, dominating the composition as it kicks out against the dog but also aims at Isabella's womb. This attack on her innocence is accompanied by violent clenching of the nutcracker: broken shells litter the damask cloth.

The force of sexual desire is felt with curious intensity in Millais's small painting *The Bridesmaid* (1851) [39], in which a young girl wearing the bridal insignia of orange blossom is seen passing a morsel of wedding cake nine times through a ring, to ensure a vision of her future spouse. This was a ritual still common in the Victorian age, according to the artist, and similar to the scramble for the bride's bouquet. Dreaming of her own nuptials, this young woman is romantically enrapt, her face lifted towards the spectator, lips parted ready for kissing. Moreover, half the canvas is filled with her cascading corn-coloured hair.

In reality, of course, loose hair was worn only by children; in womanhood it was braided or pinned up and thereafter visible only when retiring or rising. Its appearance in art has therefore an intimate, erotic significance. Millais's bridesmaid could hardly have been so 'undressed' at an actual wedding feast; she is a visual symbol of marriageability. The message is reinforced by the orange and by the phallic silver sugar caster, and by a comparison of the image with Rossetti's preliminary studies for the figure of Delia [40], the young Roman wife of Tibullus. Both young women are dreaming of their husbands, with loose hair and uplifted faces. Delia moreover is already in her nightgown, and the full composition shows Tibullus's unexpected return, bursting through the curtained door: the sequel does not need to be spelt out. It was, in my

38 John Everett Millais, Isabella, 1848–9.

view, while drawing Elizabeth Siddal as Delia in the winter of 1851–2 that Rossetti began to fall in love with her, although at first this emotion was not acknowledged; his drawings display a narrowing focus on her hair, recalling the metaphorical veil through which Chiaro 'beheld his dreams', and a strong but submerged sense of yearning.

As biographies and memoirs show, the main concern of a young Victorian girl was usually marriage, an obsession felt most acutely in families with several daughters, who spent their youth preparing, scheming and dreaming of husbands. This social reality was reflected obliquely in the 'garland of girls' artistic motif, showing attractive young women in decorative but inactive poses, hopeful of future happiness.

Once married to Effie, Millais was often in the company of her sisters Sophie and Alice, who were among the models for his haunting canvas *Autumn Leaves* (1855–6), which he described as 'a picture full of beauty and without subject' but which is in fact also a seasonal meditation on mortality. [2] This was complemented by *Apple Blossoms* [41], begun in 1856, its original title, *Spring*, indicative of the season of maidenhood and romance. In this orchard picnic, painted out of doors according to Pre-Raphaelite principles, it is easy to perceive the significance of the pink-and-white petals that promise the ripeness of apples. The eight girls, said to be eating porridge although it appears more like buttermilk, are disposed horizontally across the frame in attitudes of nubile femininity; all are innocently unaware except the figure on the far right, lying in a posture of abandonment, whose gaze meets the spectator's. Above her is poised Time's scythe, like an unsheathed sword, and a basket of cut flowers. The implicit analogy of girls as blossoms is unmistakable.

Edward Burne-Jones acquired four sisters-in-law when he married Georgiana Macdonald in 1860, and until they too married he flirted chastely with his 'wenches'. It is possible that the girls inspired Rossetti's watercolour of medieval ladies playing music, *The Blue Closet* (1856–7), since William Morris used their names in his accompanying poem. Certainly they are portrayed in Burne-Jones's watercolour *Green Summer* (1864) which, one-tenth the size of *Apple Blossoms*, also contains eight maidens sitting on the grass in a 'harmony of greens', listening to a story. Georgie, reading, is dressed in black.

Personal meaning is only part of the content of such pictures as *Green Summer*, which as a colour composition, lacking a specific narrative or subject, looks forward to the development of Aestheticism and the work of Whistler and Moore, and to images that aim at pictorial equivalents of musical melody.

39 (opposite) John Everett Millais,
The Bridesmaid, *1851.*

40 Dante Gabriel Rossetti, study for
Delia in The Return of Tibullus to Delia,
c. 1851.

41 (overleaf) John Everett Millais, Apple Blossoms (Spring), *1856–8.*

42 *Edward Burne-Jones,* The Golden Stairs, *1866–80.*

Burne-Jones returned to the theme when his own daughter Margaret approached puberty. *The Golden Stairs* (1866–80) [42] is, as the musical instruments depicted suggest, a visual harmony, perhaps influenced by Walter Pater's famous Aesthetic aphorism, published in 1873, that 'all art aspires to the condition of music'. Equally significantly, however, music was a recognized feminine accomplishment; Georgie and her sisters were skilled and delightful music-makers, a talent much cultivated in Victorian homes. And the girls descending the stairs are also marriageable maidens, 'like spirits in an enchanted dream,' wrote Fred Stephens, 'each moving gracefully, freely and in unison with her neighbours.' [3] Each is draped in chiffon that displays her soft curving limbs; all are innocently unconscious of the spectator's gaze; and they form a full half-circle on the staircase that stops abruptly as they reach the last step. What are these girls moving so gracefully towards? By implication, the answer must lie in the fulfilment of their womanhood in the missing completion of the circle.

Among the sixteen figures, Margaret Burne-Jones can be seen at the top and May Morris, daughter of Burne-Jones's closest friend and colleague, stands half-way down the stairs with a violin (in fact she played the guitar). But the pale figures, with their 'broad foreheads, deep-set eyes and fixed look', are not so much individuals as types, images of delicate femininity. They have a strange ethereal appearance, suggestive of fragile youth and wistful beauty.

This alabaster quality in *The Golden Stairs* is both aesthetic and moral; it relates to the dislike, manifest throughout Burne-Jones's work, of any display of overt, vulgar sexuality. He aimed instead to infuse his images with latent sensuousness. It is probably a mistake to think of the Victorians as sexually repressed; indeed, heightened awareness of sex is manifested throughout the century, in attempts at regulation and control. In painting it is pervasive, even – as in the case of most Pre-Raphaelite art – without the depiction of nudity. It is also apparent in the popularity of folk and fairy tales. Here innocent femininity often features with an ambivalent childishness or supernatural distance, as if to avoid direct expression of the sexual, and often violent, content of the tales, which in this period were extraordinarily popular.

43 Edward Burne-Jones, The Rose Bower *(detail) from the* Legend of the Briar Rose, *1890.*

Something of this is visible in a bed-head illustration of *The Sleeping Beauty* (1867) by the minor Pre-Raphaelite painter Henry Holiday, fitted to a red Gothick bed designed by William Burges, now in the Cecil Higgins Art Gallery, Bedford. Was this bed, painted in love's own colour, intended for a nuptial couple? The size of the bed suggests a single occupant, but the explicit eroticism of the prince's leer towards the beauty's naked breasts is too bold for a young woman's bedroom, much less a child's. Perhaps it was meant to accompany a bachelor's dreaming fantasies.

Burne-Jones, with characteristic ambivalence, was obsessed with the Sleeping Beauty theme, derived from Perrault's fairy tale and from Tennyson's romantic poem 'The Day Dream', telling of a princess asleep within an enchanted briar thicket, and awakened from virgin tranquillity by the prince's kiss. In the early

1860s Burne-Jones used the story as the basis for a set of painted tiles. A decade later he painted a three-part version, followed by a larger sequence with four panels, known as *The Briar Rose* (1890). With increasing visual complexity, although still employing shallow spaces and linear rhythms, this traces a simple narrative sequence showing the prince entering the enchanted wood, the king and courtiers asleep, a group of sleeping servant girls and finally the sleeping princess herself, in *The Rose Bower* [43].

This closely follows Tennyson's lines:

> The silk star-broidered coverlid
> Unto her limbs itself doth mould
> Languidly ever . . .
> Her constant beauty doth inform
> Stillness with love, and day with light.

The inscription attached to *The Rose Bower* reads: 'Here lies the hoarded love, the key to all the treasure that some be. Come, fated hoard, the gift to take and smite this sleeping world awake.'

By the time the picture was finished, Margaret Burne-Jones, the model for the princess, was a young married woman of twenty-four. Like many fathers, the artist was acutely unhappy at the approach of his daughter's wedding, to the scholar J. W. Mackail. As if to mark the event, he presented her with an elaborate study for *The Sleeping Princess* in gouache with gold paint, with the inscription 'EBJ to MJM 1886–88'. In this image, the princess is preserved forever in her virgin sleep. Time and the prince's kiss are arrested, as they could not be in life.

A fantasy emblematic of unsullied youthful passion was contained in Rossetti's own early poem, 'The Blessed Damozel', which for many represented the inspirational fount of Pre-Raphaelitism. The damozel is beyond death, dreaming of the approach of her earthly lover and their heavenly reunion. She has 'three lilies in her hand' and seven stars in her hair, and is simultaneously angelic and marriageable: 'Her hair that lay along her back Was yellow like ripe corn'. The wedding, she supposes, will be solemnized by God himself.

Rossetti was frequently urged to produce a pictorial version of his poem, and eventually succumbed, painting towards the end of his career *The Blessed Damozel* (1875–8). Here the damozel floats amid flowers and foliage; behind her, pairs of reunited lovers embrace; below, the heads of three cherubs are outlined in pink flame, and from the predella the earth-bound lover gazes up with desire. The model for the damozel was Alexa Wilding, whose vacant beauty is perhaps appropriate to the dreamy sentiment of the verses, although by this date Rossetti's canvases were so similar in composition and execution that there is little to distinguish one sitter from another. The youthful longing of his lines, written over thirty years previously, is hardly visible in the florid painting.

44 *Edward Burne-Jones,* The Blessed Damozel, *c. 1857–61.*

A more successful image is Burne-Jones's gouache version *The Blessed Damozel* (1860) [44], where the awkward composition is truer to the poetic feeling:

> And still she bowed herself and stooped
> Out of the circling charm;
> Until her bosom must have made
> The bar she leaned on warm.

The warm physicality of this blessed creature's bosom made these lines notorious among Victorian readers. Burne-Jones's figure — whose profile shows a distinct resemblance to that of Elizabeth Siddal, whom the artist knew at this date — is chastely painted. Her heaven floats over the clouds like a magic carpet.

45 *Dante Gabriel Rossetti, study for lovers in* The Blessed Damozel, *1876.*

The consummation of young love, expressed in passionate embrace, forms the background of Rossetti's own *The Blessed Damozel*. A veritable swarm of kissing couples is presented in the crayon study for this, dated 1876 [45], and inscribed with the verse:

> Around her, lovers, newly met
> 'Mid deathless love's acclaims,
> Spoke evermore amongst themselves
> Their rapturous new names.

The two female figures in the foreground are modelled on Jane Morris, whose love affair with Rossetti attained legendary status.

The image, however, is taken from one of his earliest works, inspired by another legend of lovers united in death. From Dante's *Inferno* came the tale of Paolo and Francesca, whose overwhelming passion led to death and bliss in hell, where Dante saw them in an eternal embrace. Alexander Munro sculpted the couple in white marble, symbols of pure physical love, and Rossetti produced a three-part picture emblematic of the theme where Francesca is given the idealized physical shape of Elizabeth Siddal. Ruskin, commenting on Rossetti's *Paolo and Francesca* [46], noted that it was a bold but 'perfectly true' reading of the text: 'The pretty – timid – mistletoe bough kind of kiss is *not* what Dante meant.' [4]

Another pair of legendary lovers, much painted in the Pre-Raphaelite mode, were of course Romeo and Juliet, whose popularity grew steadily through the nineteenth century as figures of intense romantic passion, eternally preserved in death. The moment most favoured by artists seems to have been the lovers' parting as Romeo prepares to leave from Juliet's window at dawn with the words: 'Farewell, farewell, one kiss and I'll descend.'

Ford Madox Brown's *Romeo and Juliet* (1870) [47] is highly dramatic, recalling the declamatory theatrical style of the time, as well as the artist's own liking for strong narrative themes. Juliet is half undressed, with her eyes closed in sleepy ecstasy. One can note also the echoes of earlier pictures: the circular bull's-eye glass panes as in *Paolo and Francesca,* and the bough of apple blossom, reminiscent of Millais's orchard scene. A crow or raven croaks amid the petals, however, symbolic of approaching doom.

Frank Dicksee, a relatively neglected Victorian painter who had no personal links with the artists of the Brotherhood but also worked within the Pre-Raphaelite manner, similarly echoed Madox Brown's composition in his own *Romeo and Juliet* (1884) showing the couple from within the balcony, in the muted tones of the later period. The purity of Juliet, in her bridal nightgown, is indicated by lilies to the left, and her love by passion-flowers twining the pillar. Romeo's genitals – always a tricky area in paintings where costume hose was required – are decently obscured, and the whole image is suffused with a shadowy atmosphere of romantic feeling. The urgency of young love, so powerfully felt in the early Pre-Raphaelite images, has been lost in what may be seen as the sentimental triumph of true love, just as the disturbing intensity of early Pre-Raphaelite painting has been replaced by prettier, more decorative picture-making.

46 Dante Gabriel Rossetti, Paolo and Francesca *(detail), 1862.*

47 Ford Madox Brown, Romeo and Juliet, *1870.*

Doves and Mothers

In the Victorian delineations of femininity, the ideal young wife was, in the words of Coventry Patmore's famous poem 'The Angel in the House',

> a woman deck'd
> With saintly honours, chaste and good
> Whose thoughts celestial things affect,
> Whose eyes express her heavenly mood!

and whose charming modesty, 'amiable and innocent', is devoted to connubial and domestic duties, inspiring both husband and children through 'sense and spirit sweetly mixed'.

Patmore's poem was dedicated to his wife, Emily Andrews – 'by whom and for whom I became a poet' – whose bridal portrait was painted by Millais in 1851 [49]. Patmore was a friend of the PRB, and contributed verses to their magazine *The Germ.* Millais painted Emily not with idealizing sentiment but with full Pre-Raphaelite directness in token of her integrity and constancy, the truth of the essential soul. In life, as it proved, Emily was a model wife, bearing six children, keeping house on a small income, writing children's stories and a servants' handbook, and ministering to her husband's every mood – of which there were many – with sweet self-denying patience. Sadly, she died young, before the final volume of 'The Angel in the House' was issued in 1864. Sentimentally, this kept her memory green, becoming a universal marriage gift, presented by prospective husbands, for the rest of the century.

In conjugal love, the ideal wife was gentle and devoted. In Patmore's words, 'a rapture of submission lifts her life into celestial rest' in obedience to her spouse. A comparable devotion is seen on the rounded, trusting face of the young wife

48 Ford Madox Brown,
Oure Ladye of Good Children, *1847–61.*

in Ford Madox Brown's *The Last of England* (1855) [50], showing an emigrant couple departing for Australia. The husband is anxious and gloomy, but the wife is content; in the artist's words, 'the circle of her love moves with her'. [1] One hand holds her husband's; an unseen infant is wrapped in her cloak.

Emma Hill first modelled for Madox Brown in 1848. She was young and artless, and easily seduced. In 1850 their daughter Catherine, also known as Cathy or Katty, was born, and in 1853 Emma and Ford were married in conditions of some secrecy. The artist already had an older daughter, Lucy, by his first wife, who had died in 1846.

49 John Everett Millais, Mrs Coventry Patmore, *1851.*

Emma's origins were somewhat obscure; she claimed to be a country girl, although by the 1840s her family were living in London. They were poor, and Emma was uneducated and simple in her tastes, liking new bonnets and small 'treats'. Before marriage, and while *The Last of England* was being painted, she was sent to a ladies' finishing school to acquire some middle-class refinements. As the emigrant's wife, she posed out of doors during the snowy winter of 1852–3, 'to insure the peculiar look of *light all round* which objects have on a dull day at sea'. Later, she had temporarily to sacrifice her only warm shawl so that it too could be painted outdoors on a dummy figure. [2] The finished picture is an excellent likeness of Emma's soft, round face. Madox Brown painted himself as the emigrant, oppressed by care, while little Katty was the model for the fair-haired child.

In the second part of 'The Angel in the House', the young betrothed girl is likened to a timid pet songbird who

> now withdraws, and flits about
> And now looks forth again . . .

The shy, submissive woman of early Pre-Raphaelitism was often depicted in this way, her soft fluttering heart compared with that of a bird. Rossetti described Lizzie as 'a meek, unconscious dove', an image echoed by his sister Christina in 'Listening':

> She listened like a cushat dove
>   That listens to its mate alone,
> She listened like a cushat dove
>   That loves but only one.
>
> And downcast were her dovelike eyes
>   And downcast was her tender cheek,
> Her pulses fluttered like a dove
>   To hear him speak.

Robert Browning was more astringent: in his dramatic monologue 'Too Late' a lover satirizes his rival, who 'Rhymed you his rubbish nobody read, Loved you and doved you – did I not laugh!'

50 Ford Madox Brown, The Last of England, *1855*

The image of woman as bird also expresses the timidity and obedience of the tamed animal. 'After all, it is a very questionable kindness to make a pet of a creature so essentially volatile', ran the quotation appended to Walter Deverell's picture *A Pet* [51] when it was first exhibited in 1853. Intended only as a comment on the prevalent Victorian practice of keeping cage birds, the text and image also evoke questions about the 'keeping' of young women within the domestic enclosure of the home.

51 *Walter Howell Deverell*, A Pet, *1853.*

52 *Walter Howell Deverell*, The Grey Parrot, *1853.*

Like Rose in 'The Gardener's Daughter', the young woman in *A Pet* stands in 'half light, half shade' in the doorway leading to a sunlit garden. Her face is so close to the birdcage that she appears to be kissing the bird within, although she is probably feeding it, from the cup in her hand, with seed placed on the tongue – a contemporary practice also recorded, with strong erotic awareness, in Rossetti's poem 'Beauty and the Bird'. In *A Pet* another bird – whether pigeon, parrot or dove – rests on his cage on the floor, while a third perches in the girl's chignon: both are safe through her protective presence from the curly-coated dog who pants on the cool tiles. Metaphors of confinement, protection and trusting tameness abound: who is the true 'pet' here?

It has been suggested that in this image Deverell was rehearsing the well-known relationship between the 'dove-like' Elizabeth Siddal and Rossetti, whose 'pet' she became. [3] It is more likely that the inspiration was general rather than personal, coinciding with stirrings of discontent, in the middle years of the century, with the traditional confinement of the female role to the domestic sphere. However, new evidence indicates the possibility of a romantic attachment between Lizzie and Deverell, and elements of this may be contained in the image, although the model for *A Pet* was Eustatia Davy, whom Deverell painted several times. An attractive portrait, simply titled *Eustatia* (1853), is now in the Tate Gallery in London. She was also the model for the quiet, solitary girl in *The Grey Parrot* (1853) [52] where the bird perches tamely as its neck is tickled. A breeze lifts the curtain at the open window, but neither bird nor woman shows any desire to escape; the book on her lap is a volume of verse, which unfortunately cannot be identified as Patmore's as yet unpublished hymn to the angelic spouse.

The representation of woman as bird remained a popular theme, as Rebecca Solomon's watercolour *The Wounded Dove* [53], exhibited in 1866, indicates, with its further associations of feminine tenderness and vulnerability. Here the single female figure, in a shallow space with Chinese accessories in the background, presents a striking blend of early Aesthetic imagery with standard metaphors of Victorian womanliness.

The young, solitary woman as a favourite motif of Pre-Raphaelite art is frequently interpreted as purely decorative. Without denying the simple visual attractiveness of such images, it is worth noting that they were produced within a culture with prescriptive ideas about relations between the sexes and in particular the dependency of women. In Victorian middle-class society, women waited to be asked. Despite the advances of romantic passion, the female role remained passive, since a proposal of marriage retained its earlier contractual nature, allowing a rejected fiancée to sue for breach of promise and placing an obligation on men to support their wives. There were few opportunities for middle-class women to work, and marriage remained a girl's main goal; hers was the blushing modesty of a flower waiting to be picked.

Hence, in my view, the popularity of images of solitary girls, patiently waiting

53 *Rebecca Solomon,* The Wounded Dove, *1866.*

54 *John Everett Millais,* Waiting, *1854.*

for their princes to appear. These images are often small, 'unimportant' pictures, but they testify to a constant theme. The well-known image of Shakespeare's heroine *Mariana* (1851) [1], depicted by Millais as she rises from her embroidery with a back-stretching gesture of unfulfilment is perhaps the most famous. The quiet, pretty girl in lilac dress and pink bonnet sitting on the steps of the stile in the same artist's *Waiting* (1854) [54] is painted with less intensity and seems at first sight to be a decorative addition to an attractive rural scene. But the title is significant, as is the girl's position between the sunny meadow and the dappled light of the inviting wood beyond, to which the stile provides entry. She is on the threshold of a new experience.

Who is the young woman waiting for? The model for this picture was Annie Miller, who had been left under Pre-Raphaelite protection to await Holman Hunt's return from the Holy Land. Like Emma Hill, she was learning to be a lady, and earning pin-money from posing, under the moral guardianship of Frederick Stephens. 'She is a good little girl and behaves herself properly', reported Millais in May 1854. [4]

At the same period, Millais and Effie were also waiting for their reunion, unable to meet or correspond while the legal application to annul her marriage to Ruskin on the grounds of non-consummation was in progress; these were long months which Effie spent at her parents' home in Scotland. It was not until July 1855 that Millais and Effie were married at last.

Several other causes frequently delayed marriage, for social convention decreed that couples should possess a competence before setting up house and starting a family. It could take many years to establish a secure income — a difficulty felt especially by artists, whose earnings were seldom assured — and this meant that long engagements were a widely deplored but common feature of the age. Late marriage was also widespread, and the figure of the forty-year-old bachelor retiring from a military or colonial career to seek or claim a patient bride was not unusual.

During a long engagement, the beloved was expected to remain true and faithful, a recurrent theme in the work of Arthur Hughes, a painter who was more a follower than a leader of the Pre-Raphaelite movement, and for whom the subject may have had personal significance. Hughes's small oil study known as *Amy* from the mid-1850s, shows a solitary woman in lilac dress and stole looking at her name carved in the bark of a tree. The image recalls the beech tree that opens the second book of 'Angel in the House', in which a carved name

55 *Arthur Hughes*, April Love, *1855*.

    grows there with the growing bark
  And in his heart it grows the same.

In Hughes's *The Long Engagement* (1854–9), intended perhaps as a companion piece, the name 'Amy' is overgrown with ivy, symbol of clinging devotion and memory, and the young woman clasps the hand of her weak-faced fiancé, who

can clearly offer little hope; at their feet a silky black spaniel is sentimentally expressive of loyalty. The picture is awash with pathos despite the clarity with which the natural setting is painted. Dog roses echo the single bloom in the girl's hair.

The figure of Amy was probably modelled on Hughes's wife, his 'early and true love' Tryphena Foord, whom he married in 1855, soon after the completion of his most famous image of a betrothed couple, *April Love* (1855) [55]. This shows a brief quarrel between lovers, based on the perennially popular song from Tennyson, 'Tears, idle Tears'. 'The girl is just between joy and pain' wrote Ruskin ecstatically; *'of course* her face is unintelligible, all a-quiver – like an April sky'. [5] Scattered petals suggest the quarrel, ivy the true constancy.

Similar themes, involving young couples at tender moments, were among Millais's most popular works: *A Huguenot on St Bartholomew's Day* (1851–2), *The Proscribed Royalist 1651* (1852–3), and *The Black Brunswicker* (1859–60). A similar but less sentimental subject was *The Order of Release 1746* (1852–3) [56]. Also historical, this depicts a Jacobite rebel captured by soldiers after the battle of Culloden, whose release has been triumphantly obtained by his loyal Highland wife, poor and barefooted but full of dignity. Again, the dog underscores the theme of devotion, and from the way the wounded husband rests his head on her shoulder with grief and gratitude it seems that this is the type of wifely woman of whom Ruskin wrote when commending Sir Walter Scott's heroines for their 'infallible sense of dignity and justice, fearless, instant and untiring self-sacrifice'. [6]

In his influential essay 'Of Queens' Gardens' (1865), Ruskin set out his pre-scription for true femininity. The ideal woman was 'a gentle angel, bringing cour-age and safety'. Home was 'the place of peace . . . shelter from all terror, doubt and division . . . wherever a true wife comes, this home is always round her.'

Originally, Anne Ryan posed for the figure of the Highland wife, but the final painting was done in the spring of 1853 from Effie, ironically still at this date the unhappy, unloved wife of Ruskin. Effie declared the subject 'quite Jacobite and after my own heart', in allusion to her Scottish origins, but it also foreshadowed her own lifelong loyalty to Millais, whose career she nurtured and promoted for the rest of the century. It is above all an image of womanly comfort and constancy, conveyed through the wife's calm expression and encircling arms, within which both husband and child incline for love and support. *The Order of Release 1746* was immensely popular; when shown at the Royal Academy in 1853 a policeman was installed to keep the crowd moving. Later, when Effie's application for release from marriage was public knowledge, comments on the title were more sarcastic.

This image of motherhood is of course traditionally depicted within the Christian iconography of Madonna and Child, of which several Pre-Raphaelite versions were produced, although the motif was never as popular as the

56 John Everett Millais, The Order of Release 1746, *1852–3.*

religious influences on the movement might have suggested. Elizabeth Siddal tackled the subject several times, in a small stable-scene *Nativity* (*c.* 1855) showing the Virgin with a shapeless bundle, attended by a green-robed angel, and in a quietly glowing blue-and-red *Madonna and Child* (*c.* 1855).

More original than these, however, is her small square watercolour, *The Ladies' Lament* (1856) [57], illustrating the Scottish ballad 'Sir Patrick Spens'; this shows a group of women and children on the shore looking out to sea, where their men have been drowned. (The artist owned a copy of Walter Scott's *Minstrelsy of the Scottish Border*, and at one time planned to illustrate several ballads, whose titles she had marked in her volume.) *The Ladies' Lament* is attractively painted in pastoral tones and soft brush strokes, and its rough composition of a landscape with figures is unusual. Even more striking is the fact that the noblewomen of the ballad, with their fine clothes and gold combs, have been transformed into young mothers waiting on the beach.

'In idea the children are modern English', wrote Madox Brown of his Madonna in *Oure Ladye of Good Children* [48], defending it against charges of archaism and popery. 'They are washed, powdered, combed and bedgowned and taught to say prayers like English Protestant babes . . . to look at it too seriously would be a mistake.' [7] Perhaps he meant it should not be read solemnly, for the picture is certainly serious, celebrating gentle maternity and domesticity. Originally called *Oure Ladye of Saturday Night*, it explicitly compares the mother of Christ with contemporary motherhood, through the then familiar practice of a weekly bath in bowl or basin – bathrooms not yet being regular features in most homes. Bringing secular and sacred meaning together elevates everyday motherhood to an ideal heavenly plane, in a very Victorian manner. Madox Brown's approach, however, is not typically mawkish.

Oure Ladye of Good Children was reworked several times, ending in 1861 as a watercolour with pastel and gold paint. As well as an idealized, Italianate image of maternity, it also reflects Madox Brown's strong family affections. One night in 1855, when his son Oliver was six months old, a domestic tiff caused Brown to sleep on the sofa (where, incidentally, he dreamt of dining with Ruskin, 'who boasted that he had got one child out of his late spouse, whatever the slanderous world might say'). Waking, Brown went to look 'at Emma and Oliver asleep. Saw him trying to get the breast in his sleep. Poked it into his mouth and slipped out of the room again.' [8] The next day the quarrel was over.

Madox Brown's unfinished *'Take Your Son, Sir!'* (1851–7) [58] forms a modern-life complement to *Oure Ladye of Good Children*. 'It is but a simple study of Mrs Madox Brown and infant', remarked a critic when the canvas was first seen after the artist's death. 'Yet the imaginative realism carries us into the essential heart of things [where] the enthroned mother, her head haloed by the great mother-symbol of the mirror . . . becomes the type image of life.' The infant symbolizes the 'miraculous fusion of spirit' while in the mystic mirror 'mother and father meet in worship of the child.' [9]

57 *Elizabeth Siddal*, The Ladies' Lament, *1856.*

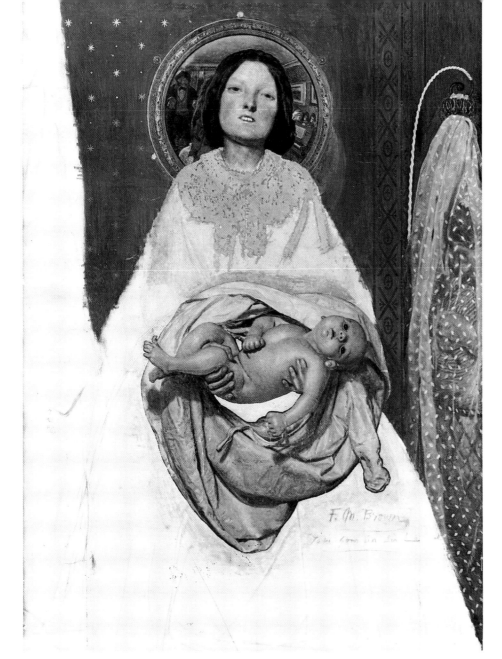

58 Ford Madox Brown, 'Take Your Son, Sir!' (detail; unfinished), 1851–7.

59 Dante Gabriel Rossetti, The Visitation, 1861.

Started in 1851, shortly after Cathy's birth, the canvas was continued in 1856 when Emma's second son Arthur was born, the beautifully realized baby held firmly in his mother's hands being painted when Arthur was a few months old. The child's death the following year may have made the subject too painful to complete. Partly because of its unfinished state, 'Take Your Son, Sir!' has in fact been subject to conflicting interpretations, including one based on a reading of the title that sees the baby as illegitimate. The painting certainly contains ambiguities, but was more likely intended as a straightforward celebration of maternity and of the first-born son, a matter of some Victorian paternal pride. 'Sir' was an old-fashioned but still current form of conjugal address.

Other births in the Pre-Raphaelite circle were sometimes represented in art, as were proud portraits of sons and daughters. A rare image of pregnancy is found in a stained-glass depiction of The Visitation [59] designed in 1861 by Rossetti for church windows at Selsley in Gloucestershire. Marriage and fatherhood prompted the formation, in this same year, of the partnership later known as

Morris & Co., which initially brought together Rossetti, Burne-Jones, Madox Brown, Morris, Hughes and others in a new version of the Brotherhood.

In 1861, when *The Visitation* was designed, several of the Pre-Raphaelite wives were pregnant. Rossetti modelled his image of the Virgin on the expectant Jane Morris (who also appears at this date in an *Adoration* by Burne-Jones). In the stained-glass cartoon and the window, the unborn Christ child and his cousin St John are shown glowing through their mothers' garments.

The devoted mother and wife as helpmeet remained a standard motif in life as well as in art; women were expected and willing to assume a supportive role. Georgie Burne-Jones brought her wood-engraving tools to married life, which Ruskin commended. 'I can't imagine anything prettier or more wifely than cutting one's husband's drawings on the woodblock – there is just the proper quality of echo in it', he wrote, 'and it will not, I believe, interfere with any motherly care or duty . . . Keep your rooms tidy and baby happy and then after that as much wood work as you've time and liking for.' [10]

This theme can be compared with that of Frank Dicksee's *Harmony* (1877) [60], painted some sixteen years later, featuring a young couple in what had by now become the requisite medieval dress for all poetic subjects. The subject is symbolic of partnership, and the young woman's music – played on an organ decorated with painted scenes – represents the harmonious qualities of true wifehood. The same theme is repeated in the stained-glass image of Madonna and Child, and in the glow of warm light that infuses the atmosphere, a glossy tone that echoes the idealization of the image.

To compensate for her dependent role, the 'true wife' was allocated moral superiority. 'A man should be chastened by a woman's love, strengthened by her courage and guided by her discretion', wrote Ruskin in 1871, elaborating on the theme of his 'Of Queens' Gardens'. [11] The same message is contained in Burne-Jones's portrait of Georgie [22] and rehearsed again in his great picture, also her favourite, *King Cophetua and the Beggar Maid* (1884) [61]. Here the maid, her delicate body draped in symbolic rags to reveal her modest, even vulnerable soul, is raised high above the reverent king, who bows in humble acknowledgement of her spiritual beauty and goodness, and in homage too to Tennyson's lines:

> As shines the moon in clouded skies,
> She in her poor attire was seen . . .
> So sweet a face, such angel grace,
> In all that land had never been:
> Cophetua swore a royal oath:
> 'This beggar maid shall be my queen.'

This is the very emblem of the angelic 'true wife'.

60 Frank Dicksee, Harmony, *1877.*

61 Edward Burne-Jones, King Cophetua and the Beggar Maid, *1884.*

Fallen Magdalens

The obverse of the dove-like maiden and angelic wife, in feminine representation, was the 'fallen woman': the seduced girl, adulterous wife, kept mistress, courtesan, harlot, or common prostitute. She stood for illicit sexuality, immorality, vice and lust – the opposite of pure, idealized, romantic love sanctioned by church, state and family.

Prostitution itself was defined, in the mid-century, as 'the great social evil', a scourge which threatened to undermine society. It is difficult to find a rational explanation for this moral panic, since in reality prostitutes – vulnerable, outcast women from the lowest economic rank – posed no threat to the power structures of the day, but were indeed society's victims, at risk themselves from violence and disease. Nevertheless, the anxiety of the age was turned on the supposed hordes of 'circulating harlotry' that gathered on the streets, particularly in London's fashionable West End, in search of clients.

Urban and commercial expansion caused profound changes and problems during this period, as the working population increased without housing or sanitation keeping pace; fear of the mob and of infection assailed the emergent middle class. Prostitution in this context was viewed metaphorically as a plague akin to the cholera and typhus that periodically surged through the slum districts and threatened the more salubrious areas. It was described in terms of pestilence and squalor, contamination and corruption. Filth and vice became synonymous, and whores were seen as festering sores on the body of society.

62 *William Holman Hunt*, Il Dolce Far Niente, *1860.*

This imagery was potent even when individual women were regarded as more sinned against than sinning. It was also immensely fascinating and alluring, because of the sexual desire that lay at the core of the 'problem', although opinions were divided as to whether the key factor was male lust or female vanity and sloth; many girls were thought too willing to trade their virtue for the promise of finery and easy living.

It is now felt that Victorian prudery in sexual matters was not so much repression as regulation, lest debauchery flood out uncontrolled. And it may be that the reason why so much Victorian art appears today as lightly disguised eroticism or soft, submerged pornography dignified by 'high art' connections, is that it formed part of the process of negotiating this difficult and disturbing terrain: art provided an approved way of articulating questions of sex.

The representation of immorality in art was determined by both social and aesthetic aims, which included reference to all forms of sexual transgression by women – male immorality is seldom portrayed – within a relatively restricted span of subjects, drawn mainly from religious and literary sources. In this area, a perennially popular figure was Margaret or Gretchen, the seduced woman in Goethe's *Faust.*

In *Gretchen and Mephistopheles in Church* (1848) [63], one of several early ink drawings on the theme by Rossetti, Gretchen is shown in the cathedral with Mephistopheles, with the accompanying rubric: 'Margaret, having abandoned virtue and caused the deaths of her mother and brother, is tormented by the Evil Spirit at Mass, during the chant of *Dies Irae*'. To stress her fallen state, a 'good', pious, soberly dressed girl is placed prominently to the left.

Joanna Mary Wells, however, presented her unfinished *Gretchen* [64] as a fresh-faced country lass – presumably before her fall, since without the title it would be difficult to interpret this image as illustrative of immorality. A classic strand in Victorian accounts of prostitution was that of rural innocence drawn into urban depravity through seduction, abandonment and despair, while the corrupting force of the city was a frequent subsidiary theme in representations of the subject.

Among other artists who handled the same theme from *Faust* was James Tissot who early in his career, in 1860–1, produced a distinctly Pre-Raphaelite series of seven images from Goethe's text ranging from *La Rencontre de Faust et de Marguerite* to two versions of *Marguerite à l'église*. In 1870 Julia Margaret Cameron produced a photographic version of Gretchen as a penitent figure, although the image is not readily distinguishable from her other soft-focused depictions of loose-haired girls.

63 Dante Gabriel Rossetti, Gretchen and Mephistopheles in Church, *1848.*

64 (right) Joanna Mary Wells (née Boyce), Gretchen, *1861.*

65 *William Holman Hunt*, The Hireling Shepherd, *1851.*

The members of the PRB were intrigued by the subject of the fallen woman, and later quarrelled over who had been the first to approach the theme. Holman Hunt tackled it boldly, in some of the most memorable if not the most attractive of Pre-Raphaelite paintings. *The Hireling Shepherd* (1851) [65] his first picture of contemporary life, shows a young country couple neglecting their agricultural duties for imminent sexual dalliance. Painted in strong, coarse colours with no concessions to pastoral romanticism, the picture shocked contemporary sensibilities; later Hunt asserted a hidden allegorical meaning about the duties of the clergy towards their straying flocks, but this is unconvincing. The picture is a depiction of lust, vanity and brazen insolence: the young shepherd is leering and the shepherdess is no rosy-cheeked innocent but a shameless hussy.

The model for the shepherdess was a Surrey girl, Emma Watkins, whose acquaintance Holman Hunt made in the fields. At around the same time, he discovered the stunning Annie Miller in the slums of Chelsea, and set in motion his plan to rescue her from inevitable degradation. The first step was to ask her to pose as the kept woman in *The Awakening Conscience* (1853) [67]. In a letter to *The Times*, Ruskin explained its subject:

> The poor girl has been sitting with her seducer; some chance words of the song 'Oft in the stilly night' have struck upon the numbed places of her heart; she has started up in agony; he, not seeing her face, goes on singing, striking the keys carelessly with his gloved hand . . .

> There is not a single object in that room – common, modern, vulgar . . . but it becomes tragical, if rightly read . . . the torn and dying bird upon the floor; the gilded tapestry . . . the picture above the fireplace, with its single drooping figure – the woman taken in adultery; nay, the very hem of the poor girl's dress . . . has story in it, if we think how soon its pure whiteness may be soiled with dust and rain, her outcast feet failing in the street . . . I surely need not go on? [1]

The Awakening Conscience was painted in a specially hired room in St John's Wood, an area of London where such love-nests were supposedly located. To avoid criticism of the 'immoral' subject, at a time when art was still expected to be uplifting, it depicts the moment of the kept woman's remorse, and the possibility of redemption. And it was, no doubt, intended as a warning to Annie Miller [66] of what the future might hold for a pretty working-class girl without much moral sense.

Rossetti's *Found* (1854–81) [68] outlines a more pessimistic conclusion, foreshadowed in Ruskin's comments about the dust and dirt awaiting the outcast woman. In the artist's own words, *Found*

> represents a London street at dawn . . . a drover has left his cart . . . (in which stands baa-ing a calf tied on its way to market) and has run a little way after a girl who has passed him . . . and she, recognizing him, has sunk under her shame upon her knees . . . [2]

67 William Holman Hunt,
The Awakening Conscience, *1853.*

66 Unknown photographer, Annie Miller, c. *1860.*

The woman is the drover's former sweetheart, now a prostitute, as proclaimed by her sprigged gown and silken shawl, which contrast strongly with the man's working smock and gaiters. Desire for fine clothes was widely seen as the bait that lured into vice servant girls discontented with the plain, hard-wearing garments appropriate to their rank. This fallen woman is beyond redemption, and in Rossetti's accompanying poem she cries out in anguish: 'Leave me – I do not know you – go away!'

Found proved a difficult subject and Rossetti never finally completed the canvas. The idea was conceived at an early date, and Ellen Frazer, the Munros' maid, may have sat for a preliminary study of the woman's head. Painting began in 1854 and continued in 1858 when Rossetti met Fanny Cornforth, a real prostitute, who accosted him, according to her own account, at a firework display in a public pleasure garden. Immediately, Rossetti asked her to his studio, 'where he put my head against the wall and drew it for the head in the calf picture'. [3] This drawing, the study for *Found* [69] from 1858, shows Fanny's features in an expression of shame and regret, as appropriate to the subject. Fanny's actual appearance, and her lack of shame, are visible in one of the few surviving photographs of her, showing her wearing the same earrings as in the drawing [70]. The similarity of the pose against the mirror, which was presumably arranged by Rossetti for the photographer, suggests that Fanny may well have been proud of her role in *Found.*

Rossetti's image of the prostitute was based partly on his own observations in London and partly on his much earlier reading of William Bell Scott's poem 'Rosabell', detailing the history of a fallen girl. In 1857 these influences combined in Rossetti's sombre watercolour *The Gate of Memory*, seemingly closely linked to a scene from the poem in which the shamed woman in a dark alley watches a group of dancing children. Their youthful movement and flower-crowned happiness represent her own lost innocence, as perhaps she suggests their potential future in such squalid surroundings. Between the figures a large rat disappears into a sewer, a symbolic representation of prostitution's moral filth and contagion.

Rossetti's meeting with Fanny altered this rather abstract view of prostitution and his poem 'Jenny' was a possible result of this revaluation. 'Lazy, laughing, languid Jenny' is neither ashamed nor depraved, but simply 'fond of a kiss and fond of a guinea', and physically exhausted by her trade; she is grateful to a client – a young student not unlike the PRB members – who simply watches her sleep. Despite his sympathy, the student cannot entirely revise his received ideas, looking on her fair form as a snare that belies her 'desecrated mind where all contagious currents meet'.

Fanny was a fine-looking woman, in the memory of William Rossetti, and from the late 1850s she became principal model for Rossetti's 'Venetian' figures. These were half- and three-quarter-length females surrounded by flowers and finery – his 'visions of carnal loveliness', such as *Fazio's Mistress*. Gradually,

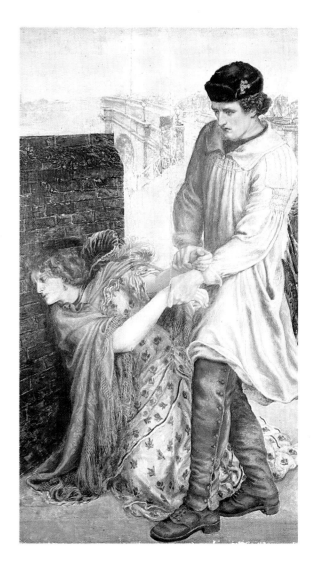

68 *Dante Gabriel Rossetti,* Found *(detail),* *1854–81.*

69 Dante Gabriel Rossetti, study for
Found, 1858.

70 W. and D. Downey, photograph of
Fanny Cornforth, 1863.

these replaced his 'types of female excellence' and moral purity.

The first of these carnal beauties was the notorious *Bocca Baciata* (1859) [72], commissioned by George Boyce and painted from Fanny, whom Boyce thought 'jolly and engaging'; for a while he and Rossetti vied for her favours. The title is taken from a bawdy tale by Boccaccio concerning a woman with many lovers, whose 'much-kissed mouth' renews its freshness, in a clear denial of the idea of sexually active women becoming 'soiled'. This boldness provoked Swinburne to comment that the picture 'is more stunning than can be decently expressed', [4] while Holman Hunt compared it to imported pornography, saying that it displayed 'gross sensuality of a revolting kind'. [5] Perhaps only the woman's direct gaze can now be interpreted as immodest, but certainly the image is unmistakably one of sexual allure.

72 (right) Dante Gabriel Rossetti, Bocca Baciata, 1859.

There followed a long sequence of similarly luscious females, and in the context of the Victorian representation of femininity, the appearance in art of such full-throated women with luxuriant hair and gorgeous, jewelled accessories signals an implicit recognition of the female sexuality that well-brought-up women were not supposed to feel; conventional wisdom taught that, for ladies, sex was a duty rather than a pleasure. This was, of course, not necessarily true in practice, but the representation of figures shamelessly exhibiting their physical charms was an innovation in Pre-Raphaelite art, and was deeply shocking to many.

To indicate the erotic meaning, the word 'bower' was commonly employed as a poetic euphemism for 'bed'. Any painting with 'bower' in its title is likely to be an erotic feminine image; the connection is made clear in Rossetti's poem 'Song of the Bower':

What were my prize, could I enter thy bower
  This day, tomorrow, at eve or at morn?
Large lovely arms and a neck like a tower,
  Bosom then heaving that now lies forlorn.

71 *Dante Gabriel Rossetti,* Blue Bower, *1865.*

When the poet's *Blue Bower* [71], painted in 1865, was exhibited in 1883, a prim middle-class young woman whose father was physician to the Pre-Raphaelite circle saw Fanny standing boldly before the image of 'the brilliant coloured lady in a green dress, with blue tiles and passion flowers behind her head', and commented acidly that in real life the model was 'a nasty, common-looking creature'. [6] Notions of morality and propriety were firmly linked, and she believed the disreputable Fanny to have replaced Lizzie in Gabriel's affections. Even Holman Hunt, despite his disapproval of such presentations of 'gross sensuality', was drawn to similar imagery. This may have been partly a question of rivalry, as he was always conscious of others' commercial and critical success, but it also relates to his own very strong pull towards sexual imagery, as *The Hireling Shepherd* and *The Awakening Conscience* indicate. It seems evident that he regarded feminine physicality as a snare; his presentations are consistently more coarse and less appealing than those of Millais or Rossetti, for example.

And the figure in his *Il Dolce Far Niente* (1860) [62] appears to me to belong in this context of sexual allure, even though she was probably meant as an image of nubile maidenhood.

Despite the domestic setting, the young woman in *Il Dolce Far Niente* looks bold and brazen. The directness of her gaze makes the spectator uncomfortable, almost as if accosted. Although the artist doubtless intended to stress her respectability, she displays her engagement ring suggestively, with more than a hint of vulgar anticipation. And the title, usually translated as 'Sweet Idleness', refers to the contemporary belief that girls were naturally empty-headed and pleasure-loving. It has been said that the picture was inspired by Hunt's critical reaction to Annie Miller's pursuit of pleasure and disinclination to work – he lectured her on his own discipline and self-denial – and it is probable that she was the original sitter for the figure, although it was finished from a professional model some years later. (Annie achieved her ambition of a successful marriage, to a cousin of Lord Ranelagh, and thus entered the world of approved idleness: the Victorian upper classes did not believe in the ethic of hard work.)

It is also possible to read Hunt's picture as a comment on the commercial nature of the mid-Victorian 'marriage market', whereby young ladies were perceived as selling themselves for the best offer in terms of income and status they could attract; feminine charms and accomplishments were seen as legitimate inducements in this transaction. Some such submerged meaning, in the purchase of comfortable idleness through a wedding ring, may be contained in the painting, and account for the similarities between *Il Dolce Far Niente* and *The Awakening Conscience*, where a comparable relationship is seen as morally reprehensible. Several contemporaries believed, with William Morris, that in the prevailing state of society, most marriages were 'but legalised prostitution'.

These were difficult areas for pictorial art. A more acceptable type of fallen woman, in whom redemption was paramount, was of course Mary Magdalene, the shadowy figure from the New Testament who became a sort of patron saint to fallen women and a symbol of repentance for sexual transgression. Prostitutes were sometimes poetically referred to as 'magdalens', while houses of reclamation, often run by Anglican nuns like Maria Rossetti, were known as magdalen homes'.

In 1857, when he was obsessed with the fallen woman theme, Rossetti painted *Mary Magdalene Leaving the House of Feasting*, showing her with bare feet, loose hair and a crown of flowers; this was drawn from Annie Miller, during one of her attempts to escape Hunt's jurisdiction. The following year the same character is seen in *Mary Magdalene at the Door of Simon the Pharisee* (1858) [73], now with Ruth Herbert's features. Rossetti's third attempt, twenty years later, is a soft, glamorized but rather vulgar green and gold image, which may be based on earlier drawings of Ruth Herbert. It shows a female face with full throat and loose hair, with Christmas roses in the background. This is similar in conception to Fred Sandys's much earlier image of *Mary Magdalene* (1858–60)

73 (left) Dante Gabriel Rossetti, Mary Magdalene at the Door of Simon the Pharisee, *1858.*

74 Anthony Frederick Sandys, illustration for If, *1866.*

[76], again dating from the period of Fanny's advent on the Pre-Raphaelite scene. It depicts the Magdalene in glowing colours as a pink-lipped girl holding her alabaster jar before a green-patterned background. In fact, it was Rossetti who accused Sandys of plagiarism, alleging that his treatment of the subject was directly taken from *Mary Magdalene Leaving the House of Feasting*, which it indeed partly resembles.

Although Fanny was not the model for Sandys's *Mary Magdalene* (whose identity is unknown), she did sit to him, for the figure of a girl vainly yearning for her beloved, in an illustration of Christina Rossetti's poem 'If':

> If he would come today, today,
>   today –
> Oh what a day today would be!

Unfortunately, by 1866, the date of Sandys's *If* [74], Fanny's ample figure and somewhat sulky expression did not in the least accord with the mood of the verses. The strand of hair in the mouth seems to relate rather obviously to Rossetti's earlier image of yearning desire modelled by Lizzie in *Delia*, while Sandys's fat, blowzy figure expresses no such delicate romance.

After Rossetti's death in 1882, his friend and assistant Frederic Shields was asked by Christina and her mother to design a memorial window for the church in Kent where he was buried. Chosen for his own 'personal love of Christ' as well as friendship with Rossetti, Shields unaccountably selected a design based on *Mary Magdalene at the Door of Simon the Pharisee*, which was immediately rejected by the vicar of the church as 'unlikely to inspire devotional thoughts' in his parishioners. Shields defended the image, in which the fallen woman 'tore away her ornaments to fall stripped of her pride at the Saviour's feet, changed and renewed', as very appropriate to 'an age of vanity like this', when 'the daughters of Christian England' went about 'walking and mincing in their high-heeled shoes, decked with a larger category of fripperies than the prophet enumerates, their hair curled with crimping pins in defiance of apostolic injunction'.[7] The vicar, however, decided that 'the ladies of his congregation would not be moved to cast aside their hair curlers or high-heeled shoes', and a design based on *The Passover in the Holy Family* was substituted.

Mary Magdalene was, however, elsewhere regarded as an appropriate ecclesiastical motif; one late example from the Arts and Crafts movement but clearly based on Pre-Raphaelite principles is the gesso figure *Mary Magdalene* (1903) [75], designed by Robert Anning Bell and originally placed behind the altar at Park Church, Glasgow. In this image of remorse for sexual transgression, she kneels humbly and raises her face with the ecstasy of repentance, her head haloed. She could almost as easily represent a saintly virgin, or a nubile maiden.

75 Robert Anning Bell, Mary Magdalene, *1903.*

76 Anthony Frederick Sandys, Mary Magdalene, *1858–60.*

Medieval Damozels

In protest against steamships and railroads, against textile factories and iron foundries, against the loss of revealed religion and the rise of science, the Victorian age rediscovered and re-created the Middle Ages, or rather its own romantic idea of the medieval world, drawn from the tales of chivalry and romance, peopled with kings, knights, courtly ladies and damozels, and with stirring accounts of unreal battles, quests and tournaments.

This mock-medievalism was always a make-believe world, although it produced some odd effects on actual behaviour as Victorian men and women strove to apply its ideals. The code of chivalry was, for example, seriously elaborated as the basis of the nineteenth-century English gentleman's sense of honour, and attentive courtship of married women was accepted as a legitimate form of adultery. Heraldry received a new lease of life, fake Gothick castles were built, feudal honours restored, and ancient chronicles revived.

Elizabeth Siddal's endeavour to produce a sequence of illustrations to Walter Scott's *Minstrelsy of the Scottish Border*, mentioned earlier, was part of this process. Her most successful attempt was a finished watercolour of *Clerk Saunders* (1854–7), for which the preparatory pencil drawing illustrated here [78] – and presumably composed in reverse for woodblock reproduction – is a good example of the spiky, stiff, intense early Pre-Raphaelite style.

It rehearses a familiar but slightly macabre version of undying romantic love. In the ballad, May Margaret's lover Clerk Saunders is killed by her brothers

77 Daniel Maclise, Madeline After Prayer, *1868.*

because of his low status (there are shades of Isabella and Lorenzo here); after death, his spirit appears – here wrapped in his shroud and passing ghost-like through the wall of Margaret's chamber – to appeal to his beloved:

> 'Gie me my faith and troth again,
> I wot, true love, I gied to thee' . . .
> Then she has ta'en a chrystal wand
> And she has stroken her troth thereon,
> She has given it him out of the shot window
> Wi' mony a sad sigh, and heavy groan . . .

Inside the room of a medieval-style keep, the lovers re-exchange their vows.

Other texts also inspired medievalism, Malory's *Le Morte d'Arthur*, a ragged compilation of romance tales about King Arthur, Gawain, Tristram, Lancelot, and the other Knights of the Round Table, was reissued early in the century, together with English translations of Froissart's *Chronicles* and the Welsh *Mabinogion*. Walter Scott's own narrative tales such as *The Lay of the Last Minstrel* and *Marmion* paved the way for Kenelm Digby's *Broadstone of Honour* and Charlotte Yonge's *The Heir of Redclyffe*. Archaic spellings, including obsolete Anglo-Saxon words, became all the rage. The literary revival culminated in Tennyson's *Idylls of the King*, appearing in instalments between 1859 and 1873, and retelling in verse the stories of Arthur, Merlin, Guinevere, Lancelot, Geraint, Enid and Elaine.

These legendary heroes and heroines were conceived as types for true Victorian masculinity and feminity, and as models for idealized relations between the sexes. Tennyson's chivalric figures inhabit the social world of the nineteenth-century middle class, and proved influential in shaping and upholding Victorian concepts of virile manhood and sweet, submissive womanhood. In the world of the *Idylls*, men were strengthened and sustained by women's faith and courage, or betrayed and beguiled by their falsity and enchantments.

78 Elizabeth Siddal, Clerk Saunders, 1854–7.

The transposition from modern to medieval life was a simple matter, and indeed Arthur Hughes's picture of *The Brave Geraint (Geraint and Enid)* [79], painted in 1860, simply offers yet another image of romantic courtship to set beside his *April Love* and *Long Engagement*. These two young people just happen to be in medieval costume and possess names from Tennyson's poem. 'Enid', the first *Idyll*, was written in 1856; it presents its heroine as the archetype of the loyal and loving wife, who dutifully dons 'her worst and meanest dress' in obedience to Geraint's bidding, and patiently undergoes humiliating tests and trials when he mistakenly believes her false. This self-sacrificial love and courage earn her the title 'Enid the Good', and she became instantly popular with the public; over twenty paintings based on Enid's tale were shown at the Royal Academy in the years following 1860.

Hughes's woodland scene depicts none of the unpleasant incidents from the poem, but rather a pictorial image of the lines when Enid's sweet voice first moves Geraint to love, as when the nightingale heralds the spring,

> and in April suddenly
> Breaks from a coppice gemm'd with green and red . . .
> So fared it with Geraint, who thought and said
> 'Here, by God's grace, is the one voice for me.'

Enid's lute, strewn with bluebells, must represent her song – whose theme, incidentally, is 'of Fortune and her Wheel', the subject of a major picture by Burne-Jones some years later.

79 *Arthur Hughes*, The Brave Geraint (Geraint and Enid), *1860.*

Photographers were also attracted by Tennyson's medievalism, despite the sometimes risible results of their tendency to dress models in literal replicas of chainmail and armour. During the 1870s, Julia Margaret Cameron undertook a full sequence of illustrations to *Idylls of the King,* sensibly concentrating more on poetic atmosphere than detailed rendering. Her single figure image, *And Enid Sang* (1874) [81], depicts the same moment as Hughes's painting, while *Gareth and Lynette* (1874) [80] is a misty, leafy composition which echoes Hughes's

Geraint and Enid in the reversal of the figures, and which also represents legendary romantic love. Tennyson's 'Gareth and Lynette' was published in 1872.

Arthur Hughes was one of the team assembled by Rossetti for the 'jovial campaign' in the summer of 1857 to decorate the coved ceiling of the new University debating chamber in Oxford with scenes from the *Le Morte d'Arthur*, which the Pre-Raphaelites in general preferred to Tennyson's politer version. These murals represent a more robust and authentically archaic response to medieval sources. Unfortunately, they have all but deteriorated beyond recognition. This enthusiasm for the medieval was inspired too by Ruskin's essay on 'The Nature of Gothic', and expressed through the contributions to the *Oxford and Cambridge Magazine* produced by Burne-Jones, William Morris

80 Julia Margaret Cameron, Gareth and Lynette, *1874.*

81 Julia Margaret Cameron, And Enid
Sang, *1874.*

and their university friends in partial homage to *The Germ.* Morris himself was a
serious student of late medieval art, architecture, armour, manuscript
illumination and stained glass and, as if in tribute to King René of Anjou, a ruler
proficient in all the arts, the second wave of Pre-Raphaelitism encompassed
and encouraged all forms of decorative as well as fine art.

82 Elizabeth Siddal, Lady Affixing a Pennon to a Knight's Spear, c. 1858

The masculine side of medievalism was largely concerned with battles, jousts and tourneys, with the accompanying quasi-chivalric code of military honour that permeated late-Victorian regiments and sports teams. The feminine side centred on courtly ladies, who inspired their knights to deeds of valour, and on damsels in distress. The two sides came together on the eve of battle, and a cluster of paintings on this theme from the late 1850s illustrates the simple but evocative motif of chivalrous relations between the sexes.

Elizabeth Siddal's watercolour of *c.* 1858, now known as *Lady Affixing a Pennon to a Knight's Spear* [82] should perhaps be called 'Before the Battle', showing as it does an armoured knight preparing to depart for war. Or perhaps he is going to a tournament, and the pennon in love's own colour is his lady's favour or token. The red triangle of the pennon binds the figures together, as does the lady's embracing arm, in a restful image of affectionate companionship. Unlike some medievalist images, this couple are engaged in the practical problem of nailing the pennon to the shaft, which is clearly giving the knight some trouble.

In Rossetti's *Before the Battle* (1858) [83] a red-robed lady is also affixing a pennon to a knight's spear, which suggests that the works were undertaken simultaneously, possibly in the winter of 1857—8 when Lizzie and Rossetti were in Derbyshire together. Rossetti's lady is raised above both knight and spectator, both of whom look up at her loveliness; her features, incidentally, have Lizzie's aspect. The composition is crowded, confused and over-full, but amid the busy patterning the 'separate spheres' of Victorian masculinity and femininity may be discerned. The women are weaving, carding and spinning wool; the men ride out to fight or joust, carrying the banners decorated by their ladies.

Burne-Jones's contemporary ink drawing *Going to the Battle* (1858) deploys the same theme, with three damsels bidding farewell to their knights, but with the interesting addition of a chained parrot, prevented like the women from setting out on quests and adventures. The same artist's *The Knight's Farewell* (1858) shows an embrace on the eve of departure, as does Rossetti's *Chapel Before the Lists* (1857—64); these romantic images contrast with Siddal's almost domestic scene. All these pictures were executed at a time when the artists were contemplating or negotiating the transition to married life, when the separate spheres were linked but not dissolved in matrimony.

A strong complementary theme was that of the prince or knight rescuing a damsel from distress and danger. In the inner Pre-Raphaelite circle around Rossetti, Morris and Burne-Jones in the early 1860s, the story of St George saving the princess from the dragon was immensely popular, appearing in paintings, stained glass and decorated furniture. It is, of course, a traditional pictorial motif in Western art, appearing in a number of different mythological guises, and including piety and patriotism in its meanings; in the Pre-Raphaelite versions the metaphors of masculine valour and feminine weakness are dominant.

83 Dante Gabriel Rossetti, Before the Battle, *1858.*

The story had especial significance for William Morris, who decorated a painted sideboard, now in the Victoria and Albert Museum, with scenes of St George, and supervised the production of a stained glass sequence based on the story commissioned from Morris & Co. in 1861, for which Rossetti did the designs. The tale had personal meaning too, for Morris himself rescued a real damsel from the distress of poverty and ignorance when he proposed to Jane Burden, 'discovered' in Oxford during the mural painting adventure. Jane, daughter of a stableman and probably working in domestic service, was educated to be a lady and was married to Morris in the spring of 1859. The following year the young couple moved to their enchanted 'palace of art', the newly built, quasi-medieval Red House at Bexleyheath in Kent. Later, they took the more authentic, fifteenth-century Kelmscott Manor in Oxfordshire as a summer home.

Jane was the model for the figure of *La Belle Iseult* (1858) [85] sorrowfully clasping her golden girdle in a windowless bedchamber as she yearns for Sir Tristram. Like Guinevere, Iseult's love is romantic although strictly speaking adulterous, since she is married to King Mark; in Victorian eyes she represented the tragic face of courtly love.

While working on this image, Morris is supposed to have scribbled a shy declaration to Jane: 'I cannot paint you, but I love you', and in an excess of romantic chivalry went on to marry her, despite the fact that she did not return his love. It was, however, an offer she could not refuse. The intense, oppressive details of fabric and pattern in the painting create an atmosphere appropriate to the medieval scene, and an authentically archaic sense, although Iseult and her chamber are rather strikingly reminiscent of Holman Hunt's illustration of *Godiva* (1856) [84] engraved by Dalziel for the Moxon edition of Tennyson, with which Morris was familiar. Morris's picture is sometimes mistakenly identified as 'Queen Guinevere', but the little dog asleep on the unmade bed is Iseult's emblem, a gift to her from Sir Tristram.

La Belle Iseult appears to have taken many years to complete – it is Morris's only surviving easel painting – and was not exhibited until 1896. All the more striking and significant, therefore, is the comparison with Daniel Maclise's highly medieval image from Keats of *Madeline After Prayer* [77], produced in 1868. Here Maclise, who was a noted illustrator of Tennyson within the academic tradition, selects a Gothick chamber for his damozel, with a profusion of picturesque medieval accessories – carved and painted wood, stained glass, embroidery frame, clasped books and a faintly anachronistic lute – in a composition not unlike Morris's in structure, but quite different in feeling.

Despite the unmade bed, Iseult is not presented in erotic terms, while Madeline in Maclise's painting is undressing in a sensuous manner for the spectator's delight. This is, of course, true to the poem if somewhat in conflict with the title of the painting, since this young woman's thoughts are evidently not with her prayers. The highly professional finish to Maclise's picture also contrasts with the rough quality of Morris's. *La Belle Iseult* can be viewed as more authentically

85 (right) William Morris, La Belle Iseult, *1858.*

84 William Holman Hunt, Godiva, *1856.*

86 *Jane Morris and Elizabeth Burden,*
Hippolyta, *c. 1880.*

'Pre-Raphaelite' in terms both of content and treatment, while *Madeline After Prayer* demonstrates how widespread the influence could be.

At Red House, Jane Morris entered enthusiastically into her husband's revival of ancient embroidery techniques, unpicking old pieces in order to learn how the stitches were laid. Jane, her daughters Jenny and May, and her sister Elizabeth (Bessie) Burden, all became renowned for their embroidery and supervision of this department of Morris & Co., and may be credited with much creative design, although in the interests of commercial success most of the embroidery design was ascribed to William Morris himself.

Three elaborate embroidered panels now at Castle Howard are samples of the work produced by Jane and Bessie in the 1880s. They are based on a scheme to decorate the walls of Red House with embroidered images of Illustrious Women, in homage to both Chaucer and Tennyson. Iconographically, the most unusual of the figures is *Hippolyta* [86], the mythological Amazonian leader who became Theseus' bride, here depicted as a medieval warrior-maiden with sword and spear, and a full suit of armour beneath her tapestried robe. It is a strikingly warlike pose compared with most Victorian representations of femininity and, although very decoratively wrought, serves as contrast to the somewhat passive roles to which medieval damozels were generally confined.

The story of Tristram and Iseult (also called Isoude or Isolde), a favourite Pre-Raphaelite theme from medieval sources, echoed through the nineteenth century in painting, poetry and music. Following the publication of old romance texts, Matthew Arnold produced his version of *Tristram and Isolde* in 1852, a study of nostalgic and domestic affection. In *Idylls of the King*, Tennyson betrayed the tale, presenting the relationship as shameful sin, emblematic like Guinevere's adultery of the moral decay of Camelot, or England. Wagner's opera *Tristan und Isolde* was performed in 1859, and Swinburne's verse drama *Tristram of Lyonesse* appeared in 1880, exalting the lovers' passion and exulting in its sinfulness.

Among the earliest productions of Morris & Co. was a stained-glass window sequence telling Malory's story, with designs by Rossetti, Burne-Jones, Madox Brown, Arthur Hughes, Val Prinsep and William Morris. Morris's own design, *The Recognition of Sir Tristram* or *Tristram and Iseult in the Garden* (1862) [87] shows Iseult's dog (for which Malory used the archaic term 'brachet', meaning bitch) recognizing the wounded Tristram before Iseult does.

The same moment is depicted in Marie Spartali Stillman's version *Sir Tristram and Iseult* which was hung at the Royal Academy in 1873. In the dramatic atmosphere of the scene and deep, dense green of the tree-filled garden it shows the influence of her training with Madox Brown, while in the awkward, unsophisticated composition it pays homage to Pre-Raphaelite principles. The lilies beside Iseult suggest that this artist believed in the purity of her heroine's love.

88 (overleaf) Edward Burne-Jones, The Arming and Departure of the Knights of the Round Table on the Quest of the Holy Grail, *c. 1890.*

87 William Morris (Morris and Co.), The Recognition of Sir Tristram, *1862.*

The large tapestry showing *The Arming and Departure of the Knights of the Round Table* (c. 1890) [88] designed by Burne-Jones for a vast *Holy Grail* series produced by Morris & Co., shows a more conventional rendering, and returns to the 'going to battle' theme, with the damsels meekly handing weapons and armour – shield, sword, helmet and lance – to the heroic knights on horseback. Here the difference between masculine and feminine roles is simply but evocatively displayed.

Millais was less frequently attracted by medievalism than other members of the PRB, although he chose other historical settings, and thus *The Knight Errant* (1870) [89] is something of an aberration in his work. In life, of course, Millais had acted out this part by rescuing Effie from the bonds of a marriage without love or passion. Others might not see John Ruskin as a dragon, but in his wife's eyes he had almost consumed her youth and innocence.

The damsel in distress in *The Knight Errant* is however not an idealized medieval maiden, decoratively displayed in tapestried colours; she is a mature, contemporary figure, with skin and figure suggestive of approaching middle age. The knight, by contrast, is accoutred in full fourteenth-century armour. Originally, the lady's face was turned to the spectator, but when the picture was shown at the Royal Academy it was condemned as obscene – only idealized, classical, nubile nudes were acceptable – and the artist decided that 'the beautiful creature would look more modest if her head were turned away'. [1] Later commentators have unkindly suggested that her modesty would have been better preserved had her rescuer honourably averted his eyes from her person while cutting the cords – or at least dropped his visor.

The unintended but unmistakable bondage motif, which would be disturbing if it were not so amusing, unconsciously echoes the message of much Victorian and Pre-Raphaelite imagery of womanhood. It is present, too, in Frank Dicksee's *Chivalry* (1885) [90], painted fifteen years later and showing the damozel decently clothed – although her shoulder is fetchingly bare in the manner of Maclise's *Madeline,* and suggestive of imminent dishonour. The hero, unsheathing his sword to vanquish the lust of his fallen rival, is clad in supple feathery armour of the kind popularized by Burne-Jones – it is worn too by *King Cophetua* [61] – in order to escape from the literal constrictions of the real thing, carefully reconstructed in so many mock-baronial halls but insufficiently poetic for images of rescue. The lady's gaze is turned upwards to her saviour, with an appropriate expression of gratitude and desire.

89 John Everett Millais, The Knight Errant, *1870.*

90 Frank Dicksee, Chivalry, *1885.*

Sorceresses

The closest that Pre-Raphaelite art comes to presenting femininity in wicked or ugly guise is in the delineation of woman as enchantress or witch. But even here, womanhood is almost never shown as contemptible or base, and the images of the ensnaring sorceress are as idealized and beautiful as those of the courtly lady. Burne-Jones, who made a cult of the witch figure, insisted that the woman who held men captive through her beauty should not be blamed, however immoral her action: she could not change her nature, which was a manifestation of the goddess – amoral but divine. 'Don't hate,' he wrote with reference to Maria Zambaco, 'some things are beyond scolding – hurricanes and tempests and billows of the sea – it's no use blaming them . . . No, don't hate.'[1]

Others saw the enchantress's power as magical. One early simple portrayal of a woman with supernatural skills is contained in *Sister Helen* (c. 1854) [92], Elizabeth Siddal's illustration to Rossetti's poem of the same name. The ballad was written in dialogue and first published in 1851. In it the seduced and abandoned Helen melts a waxen image while her young brother watches her faithless lover sicken and die:

> 'But he calls for ever on your name,
>   Sister Helen,
> And says that he melts before a flame.'
> 'My heart for his pleasure fared the same,
>   Little brother.'
>   (*O Mother, Mary Mother,*
> *Fire at the heart, between Hell and Heaven!*)

91 Edward Burne-Jones, The Beguiling of Merlin, 1874.

At this early date, piety decreed that even wronged ballad heroines be punished for witchcraft, and just as Rossetti's poem ends with the loss of Helen's soul to the fires of hell, so Siddal's figure clutches her throat in horror and fascination as her mannikin melts. Curiously, some twenty years later Rossetti himself prepared a sketch to illustrate 'Sister Helen', which closely echoes Lizzie's design.

Burne-Jones's first witch was also inspired by Rossetti's poem, although in his *Waxen Image* (1856) her magic arts are used to regain the lover. His second was *Sidonia von Bork* (1860) [94], based on a Gothick romance by Wilhelm Meinhold, translated by Lady Wilde as *Sidonia the Sorceress* in 1849. Sidonia, a noblewoman of such beauty that all fall under her spell, is also incurably evil, killing and destroying the entire court and ruling caste of Pomerania. Ideas of seduction, evil and magic combined to bewitch Burne-Jones, adding 'menace to the worship of female beauty' and laying the ground for the concept of the *femme fatale*; this adolescent fantasy remained a favourite throughout his life.

On canvas Sidonia is a proud beauty. A filigree net holds her golden hair, whose colour diverts bees from their flowers; her sumptuous gown is covered with an intricate, impossible web, indicative of her wiles. In the background are glimpsed her victims, while a symbolic spider sits on the scroll bearing the artist's signature.

The model was Fanny Cornforth, whose fine face and figure belied her amoral (if not exactly evil) character. Perhaps Burne-Jones was conscious of Fanny's seductive qualities: the companion piece to *Sidonia* shows her virtuous cousin *Clara von Bork* (1860) [93] who in the story is betrayed and buried alive by the witch. In the picture Clara protectively holds a nest of fledgling doves and is assumed to represent the qualities, though not the fate, of the artist's loyal wife Georgie, who was the model. The images were painted in the year of her marriage to Burne-Jones, and in this catalogue of feminity, *Clara* belongs with the Doves and Mothers.

Other legendary witches in European literature included Morgan le Fay, King Arthur's evil half-sister, who enchanted Merlin, and Medea, whose love ensnared Jason. In the early 1860s, William Morris retold the story of Jason in verse. Medea concocts a spell with 'mystic herbs' gathered at midnight, with which to bind Jason to her:

> within her caught-up gown
> Much herbs she had, and on her head a crown
> Of dank night-flowering grasses, known to few . . .

In an early gouache by Burne-Jones, a dark figure against a dusky sky and darkened landscape is putting a strange plant to her lips. This picture, now entitled *Morgan le Fay* (1862), began as a half-figure, which was later enlarged to full-length – the joins can still be seen – and is said to be similar to a design for the figure of Medea produced in the early 1860s for tapestry and stained glass, to illustrate Chaucer's *The Legend of Good Women*.

92 *Elizabeth Siddal*, Sister Helen, c.1854.

93 Edward Burne-Jones, Clara von Bork, *1860.*

94 Edward Burne-Jones, Sidonia von Bork, *1860.*

Another enchantress was found in Arthurian legend. To complement the unquestioning obedience of Enid as the type of the true wife, Tennyson continued his *Idylls of the King* with the sorceress who bewitched 'the great enchanter' himself, the wizard Merlin, into disclosing the spell by which men could be enthralled.

> A storm was coming, but the winds were still
> And in the wild woods of Broceliande
> Before an oak, so hollow, huge and old . . .
> At Merlin's feet the wily Vivien lay.

In Malory's text, Nimuë is the name of a mysterious lady: 'Merlin fell in a dotage on the damosel that King Pellinor brought to court, and she was one of the damosels of the Lake, that hight Nimuë.' He teaches her his magical crafts, and using his own enchantment she imprisons him beneath a stone, and 'wrought so there for him that he never came out'. This was perceived as an allegory of the spellbinding powers of love and beauty.

In 1858, it is said, Burne-Jones appealed to Tennyson to change the name of his modern seductress, who tricks Merlin with her wiles, and to leave 'the ancient name of Nimuë' to the mysterious figure in *Le Morte d'Arthur*. The poet agreed, and Merlin's undoer was thus re-named the 'wily Vivien', who is shameless and serpentine:

> lissome-limbed, she
> Writhed towards him, slided up his knee and sat,
> Behind his ankle twined her hollow feet
> Together, curved an arm about his neck,
> Clung like a snake.

Vivien represents flirtatious, sexy, wicked womanhood; she is a slanderous gossip, delighting in the moral lapses of the Round Table knights, and scornful of the king's complaisant cuckoldry.

Burne-Jones hated these elements of bourgeois vulgarity imported into the old romances. His mural painting at Oxford showed Merlin – according to Coventry Patmore who visited the debating chamber while work was in progress – 'being lured into the pit by the lady of the lake' and trapped under the stone. In 1861 he produced a gouache of *Merlin and Nimuë*, and in 1874 he returned to the theme with *The Beguiling of Merlin* [91], which, although apparently based on the medieval French *Romance of Merlin*, is close to Tennyson's *Idyll* in mood and iconography: the sinuous lines of limbs, drapery and branches mesh together with the snakes entwined in Nimuë's hair. Pictorially, however, the position of the figures is reversed: Merlin now lies at the enchantress's feet, transfixed by the spell she is reciting from his ancient book of charms:

> Writ in a language that has long gone by . . .
> And every margin scribbl'd, crost and cramm'd.

95 Edward Burne-Jones, Head of Nimuë *for* The Beguiling of Merlin, *1873.*

The head of Nimuë was taken from Maria Zambaco, by whom the artist was sexually enthralled in the later 1860s and early 1870s. Prosaically, it was a familiar tale: after seven years of marriage to the capable Georgie, increasingly occupied with maternal duties, Burne-Jones met and fell for Maria, who had abandoned an unhappy marriage in Paris, and who combined the irresistible appeal of beauty, sadness and reckless vulnerability. He promised to elope, but then withdrew, retreating to the security of family and friends and leaving Maria distraught.

He felt, however, that she had his heart in thrall, like Merlin under the stone, and to exorcise his feelings he repeatedly portrayed her as a sorceress. *The Beguiling of Merlin* is his last major tribute to Maria; later he explained how Nimuë was modelled on her: 'That's the head and the way of standing and turning, and I was being turned into a hawthorn bush in the forest of Broceliande . . .'. [2] A large group of exquisite pencil studies of Maria dating from the early 1870s, testify to his infatuation, and he is said to have regarded the gouache study of the *Head of Nimuë* (1873) [95] as one of his best pieces of work, even finer than her snake-coiled, spellbinding gaze in the finished oil.

Maria's haunting profile is seen on another of Burne-Jones's witches, in a superb watercolour of *Circe* (1868) where the sorceress bends over as she pours out her potion. Warm gold and orange tones and strong linear rhythms are offset by black panthers which echo Circe's movement. Ruskin's praise of the portrayal indicates Burne-Jones's success in transforming a classical figure who elsewhere functioned as an allegory of bestiality; Burne-Jones's witch, Ruskin wrote,

> is indeed an enchantress . . . but always wonderful . . . even the wild beasts rejoice and are softened round her cave; the transforming poisons she gives to men are mixed . . . with wine, milk and corn, the three great sustainers of life – it's their own fault if these make swine of them. [3]

96 Edward Burne-Jones, Caricature of Maria Zambaco and Self, c. *1870.*

This idea of woman as elemental enchantress strengthened the theme of feminine mystery and 'otherness'; her sensuous charms were felt as enslaving – in Burne-Jones's deceptively innocuous words, 'because she is a woman and is of such a nice shape and so different to mine . . .'. [4]

97 *Edward Burne-Jones,* Laus Veneris, *1869.*

Maria is also the figure for Burne-Jones's great *Laus Veneris* (1869) [97], whose object of worship is the Venus of the Tannhäuser legend, in which a wandering knight is lost to the spells of sensual enchantment on the Venusberg. This was a favourite subject in the Pre-Raphaelite circle, first deployed by Burne-Jones in a watercolour of 1861, the year when a translation of its German ballad source was published with an illustration by Millais, and when Wagner's opera was first performed in Paris. William Morris incorporated 'The Hill of Venus' into his *Earthly Paradise* verse sequence of 1868–70, while Swinburne's erotic masterpiece 'Laus Veneris' caused a sensation when it appeared in *Poems and Ballads* in 1866.

This volume was 'affectionately and admiringly dedicated' by the author, 'to my friend,Edward Burne-Jones', and the mood of poem and painting are close:

> Her little chambers drip with flower-like red, . . .
> Her gateways smoke with fume of flowers and fire,
> With loves burnt out and unassuaged desires
> Between her lips the steam of them is sweet
> The languor in her ears of many lyres . . .

This Venus is destructive but not malignant, the personification of love's power to enslave:

> Her beds are full of perfumes and sad sound,
> Her doors are made with music, and barred round
> With sighing and with laughter and with tears,
> With tears whereby strong souls of men are bound.

98 Anthony Frederick Sandys, Medea, *1868.*

In Burne-Jones's *Laus Veneris*, Love's crown rests delicately between her legs; behind her in the shallow space is a tapestry showing Venus in her chariot hunting with Cupid, while in a frieze to the left pale knights on horseback gaze in at the maidens. On the far left is a fragment showing the goddess's birth from the waves.

Henry James described the musical maidens as 'pale, sickly and wan, in the manner of all Mr Burne-Jones's young people'; they were, however, distinctly more 'innocent' than their mistress, whom another critic saw as 'diseased' and ugly, 'gnawed away with disappointment and desire'. [5] Venus's glowing red robe, stamped with luminous gold circles, lies sensuously on her languorous limbs.

The pose of Venus echoes that of a costume study (mistakenly attributed to Rossetti) for which Fanny Cornforth sat at a date in the early 1860s, when she posed regularly for Burne-Jones. And another comparable image is that contained, significantly, in the artist's caricature of himself, the painter, gazing at his sitter, Maria Zambaco, which was drawn for her sometime in the 1870s [96] and until recently remained within her family. Like Venus, she reclines on a low seat with seductive languor.

Other artists also depicted witches and sorceresses. Fred Sandys seems to have been similarly obsessed, producing images of *Morgan le Fay* (1862), *Vivien* (1863), *Medea* (1868) [98], and *Medusa* (1875). His early image of *Morgan le Fay*

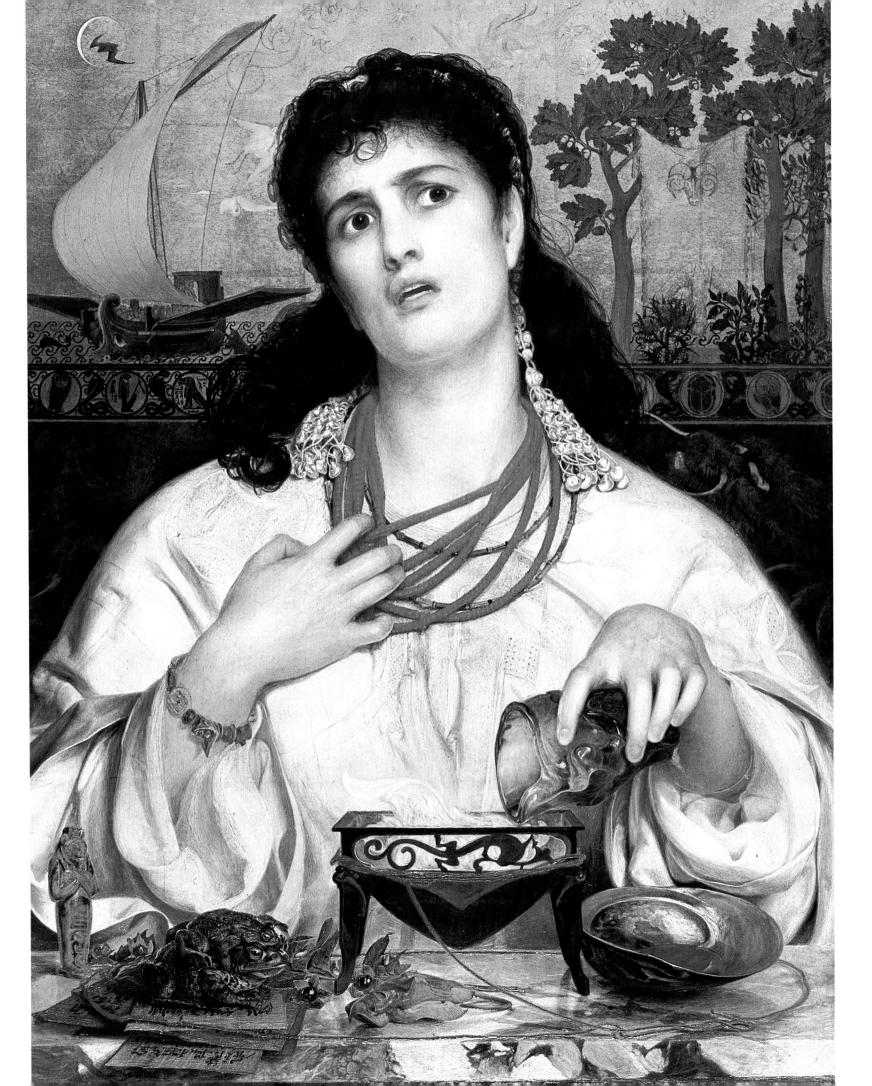

emphasizes the evil, fanatical wickedness of Arthur's nasty half-sister who makes an enchanted robe to consume him with flames. She is shown weaving both the garment of destruction, on the great loom in the background and also the spell that will bewitch it, and the violence of her desire is expressed in the harsh, abrupt lines of her gesture, and in the sinister patterning behind. Alchemical vessels and books litter the floor, occult symbols decorate her gown, and a sense of primitive animality is conveyed by the fire, the exotic carved figure and the leopard-skin apron. However, the plethora of stage props also tends to undermine the intended atmosphere of evil. Morgan's room is cramped and claustrophobic and an owl, her familiar spirit, perches atop the loom.

It is suggested that the model for Morgan was a woman of gypsy origin, now known only by the name Keomi, who was Sandys's mistress in the early 1860s. The enchantress *Medea* [98] has the same dark-haired head in a composition filled with details of witchcraft as Medea blends the ingredients of her spell. Like Rossetti's contemporary images of women, she is contained in a shallow space behind a sill that forms a barrier. Sandys's *Vivien* (1863) is a similar proud beauty, framed in peacock feathers and clad in a gold-painted magician's cloak. Rossetti, incidentally, used Keomi as a model; an attractive pencil study of her head is used for one of the attendant figures in *The Beloved* or *The Bride* (1865–6).

In the late 1860s Sandys ran off with young Mary Jones, an aspiring seventeen-year-old actress, who, on the strength of her portraits, was herself accorded a Pre-Raphaelite obituary many years later by the poet Gordon Bottomley:

> Now she is deathless by her lover's hand,
> To move our hearts and those of men not born
> With famous ladies by her living hair –
> Helen and Rosamund and Mary Sandys.

The ensnaring, even frightening effect of 'living hair' is expressed in Sandys's image of *Medusa* (1875) [100], whose gaze turned men to stone. The subject was also represented by Burne-Jones in *The Baleful Head*, but in Sandys's image Medusa is a fearsome, free-floating face with terrifying aspect and snakes coiled in her hair. On the same theme of serpentine tresses, Swinburne wrote:

> O lip curled to strike like a cobra,
> O consummate tangle of hair!

With these images, we are approaching the cruel goddess whose devotees luxuriate in pain, the Venus of whips and flagellation that provided a chief ingredient in the *fin-de-siècle* pantheon of femininity – the vampire-woman and 'poisonous queen' Dolores, Our Lady of Pain.

The painter John William Waterhouse, whose work has been assimilated into histories of the Pre-Raphaelite movement by virtue of its subject matter, produced a Medea-like witch creating spells at her cauldron in *The Magic Circle* (1886) [99], which seems indebted to Burne-Jones and Sandys in atmosphere.

100 (right) Anthony Frederick Sandys, Medusa, *1875.*

99 John William Waterhouse, The Magic Circle, *1886.*

Later, as if obsessed with sorceresses, Waterhouse portrayed *Circe Offering the Cup to Ulysses* (1891), and a finely Symbolist *Circe Invidiosa* (1892), painted in poisonous greens and virulent blues.

He also painted several pictures based on Keats's poems about bewitchment – versions of 'La Belle Dame Sans Merci' and 'Lamia'. Waterhouse's *La Belle Dame Sans Merci* 1893 [101] directly reflects its inspiration:

> I met a lady in the meads
> Full beautiful – a faery's child;
> Her hair was long, her foot was light,
> And her eyes were wild.

Waterhouse's knight is entrammelled in a skein of hair in a dark wood; he kneels awkwardly in his armour, and the mood of impending surrender is heightened, in the words of a recent critic, 'by the unmistakably erotic imagery of the lance'. [6]

Evelyn de Morgan, born in 1855, also painted witches, indicating that this subject was not restricted to the male imagination. *The Love Potion* (1903) shows a sorceress in bright yellow robes mixing a magic draught, with a black cat at her feet; on the shelves are books of spells and studies of the supernatural arts.

De Morgan's *Queen Eleanor and Fair Rosamund* [102] depicts a related theme, based on traditional sources. The tale of Fair Rosamund, beloved of Henry II and hidden away in a bower at Woodstock at the centre of a maze, tells how Queen Eleanor 'came to her by clue of thread', and destroyed her. One of the numerous re-workings of the story in poetry and painting was Swinburne's celebrated rendering in the poetic dialogue *Rosamund* (1861) in which the Queen forces Rosamund to drink a phial of poison, and which seems to have inspired de Morgan's image, with its jewelled colours and thin red line like a thread of blood between the figures. It is among the most intense and dramatic of the artist's works.

Cold, cruel, even sadistic, sorcery: as an image of femininity this was a curious feature of late nineteenth- and early twentieth-century culture, strongly present in the emerging art of cinema and owing much to the Pre-Raphaelite impulse. Maybe the enslavement of art to the representation of woman, which began in worship of loveliness and virtue, was now being expressed in terms of fetishism and mystic arts. Femininity was represented not as a metaphor for moral or individual excellence, but as sinister, sexual enchantment, emblazoned in beauty: the artist ensnared by hair.

101 John William Waterhouse, La Belle Dame Sans Merci, *1893.*

102 Evelyn de Morgan, Queen Eleanor and Fair Rosamund, c. *1888.*

Allegories and Icons

The use of the female form as a pictorial vehicle for allegory has a history as long as that of Western art; as Marina Warner has demonstrated in *Monuments and Maidens* (1985). The use of allegory was particularly vigorous throughout Europe in the latter half of the nineteenth century, and this had its impact on Pre-Raphaelitism too.

Being so widespread and varied, the use of female allegory cannot be analysed as bearing any rational relation to the actual position of women in society at a specific period:

> The female form metamorphoses from one sign to another; the body is still the map on which we make our meanings; it is chief among metaphors used to see and present ourselves . . . Meanings of all kinds flow through the figures of women, and they often do not include who she herself is. [1]

In the early phases of Pre-Raphaelite art images of women in purely allegoric or iconic form are relatively rare, if the religious pictures of the early years are perceived as biblical and subject paintings — scenes from the life of Our Lady or the saints — rather than sacred symbols in their own right. However, one of the first and plainest allegories is Holman Hunt's *The Afterglow in Egypt* (1854–63) [104], begun in Gizeh soon after the artist's arrival in the Middle East. A very similar pencil study was later converted into an etching entitled *The Abundance of Egypt*.

The symbols of plenty surrounding the figure — wheatsheaves, pigeons, water and, on the frame, pomegranates — suggest that this is an image of harvest goodness and natural fertility. Biblical allusions to Egypt as a land of plenty were familiar to Hunt and his audience, although imagery from other religions is also present — the falcon perching on the sheaf was a sacred bird of ancient

103 Dante Gabriel Rossetti, Monna Vanna, *1866.*

Egypt, while the corn-bearing woman is evidently a version of the classical Ceres or Demeter, goddess of harvest.

This is, of course, a Western European metaphor of fertility. The choice of sunset or 'afterglow' as the time depicted has its significance, to represent an ancient civilization which had passed its zenith. As Hunt soon discovered on his arrival in the Middle East, the Islamic faith did not permit allegory of the human form, prohibiting the representation of living beings in art. This, together with the veiling of women's faces, made it very difficult to obtain models, on whom Hunt, like his Pre-Raphaelite Brothers, was virtually dependent. Surprisingly, he succeeded in finding a peasant woman to pose for *The Afterglow*, but she probably contributed little to the final image, since the canvas was soon laid aside, 'what with the difficulty of getting the model day by day and the horrible trials of wind and dust even in the best places for painting in . . .'. [2] Brought back to Britain, the picture was completed in the early 1860s, not without further difficulties in the shape of 'these eternal pigeons' which, Hunt wrote in desperation, 'threaten to occupy me for the rest of my life'. [3]

104 *William Holman Hunt,* The Afterglow in Egypt, *1854–63.*

The Afterglow in Egypt is one of Hunt's more attractive presentations of the female figure, strong, sensuous and sensitive, with subtle treatment of colour to convey the glow of dusk. Ironically, its gentleness may derive from the lack of intentional moral meaning, which frequently gives his portrayals of women a harsh, aggressive edge. And Hunt was at pains to play down the allegorical interpretations of the picture when, in 1882, a French critic spelt out the theme of natural abundance in a now decayed civilization. 'The title', Hunt replied defensively, 'comes from my choice of the hour, which seemed to me the most picturesque for the figure of a girl with a singular resemblance to the old statuesque type. There is no kind or degree of mysticism in it.' [4]

In general, however, the Pre-Raphaelite artists consciously deployed the conventions of allegory, while also investing their images with other imaginative qualities and with aesthetic meaning that often almost displaces the overt symbolism. In this mode, the half-length female figure with her varied accessories became in time a tiresome Pre-Raphaelite cliché, representing anything or nothing and finishing as meaningless decoration.

In the early 1860s, Burne-Jones, who was always drawn to legendary subjects and mythological titles in order to avoid over-literal interpretation, experimented with a number of allegorical subjects which were also studies in composition and colour. The unfinished study of a figure holding a ball, which is now tentatively entitled *Hope* (1861–2) [105], is a typical example. In a similar finished work of the same date, the ball is inscribed with the medieval legend: 'If Hope were not, Heart should break'. The crystal ball was of course also an image of the future.

The model for *Hope* was Fanny Cornforth, seen here for once in a picture

105 *Edward Burne-Jones,* Hope *(unfinished), 1861–2.*

without moral message, neither as whore nor enchantress, so that it is possible to appreciate the 'fine regular features' that attracted so many admirers before her elephantine days. Because of her profession, Fanny's good qualities have been played down, although the affection between Rossetti and herself was lifelong, enduring despite his marriage to Lizzie in 1860 and his later infatuation with Jane. To others' surprise and sometimes dismay, Rossetti refused to treat Fanny as a cast-off mistress, still less as a cast-off model.

A model who sat to Burne-Jones for various allegorical figures was Antonia Caiva, an Italian immigrant to Britain, whose looks and character seem to have been appropriate for the purpose. 'She was like Eve and Semiramis,' wrote the painter, 'but if she had a mind at all, which I always doubted, it had no ideas.' [5] She had however such a fine body that she posed for many of Burne-Jones's nude figures, which he portrayed with increasing frequency in classically inspired subjects.

The 'splendour and solemnity' of La Caiva lasted a mere ten years, after which she declined into poverty and sickness, sending ill-written begging letters to her former employer from the workhouse.

It seems that models with a minimum of personality were preferred for allegorical and symbolic subjects, as 'empty vessels' chosen to carry the import of the figurative sign; faces without minds, to be filled with meaning by the artist. Certainly, one of Rossetti's favourite models for this type of painting was Alexa Wilding, whose personality did not inspire his adoration and whom he described as 'not gifted or amusing' when circumstances obliged her to dine with his mother and sister. Normally, professional models were restricted to the studio and did not necessarily meet the artist's family, but in the summer of 1873 Rossetti was living with Janey at Kelmscott Manor in Oxfordshire, where models were hard to obtain, and Alexa, who received a retainer, was invited down to pose. She had, perforce, to be treated as a guest rather than a servant; despite her dull conversation she could hardly, as Rossetti observed, be shut in a closet during mealtimes.

Alexa had a lovely face, according to Rossetti's studio assistant, 'full of quiescent, soft, mystical repose . . . but without any variety of expression. She sat like the sphinx waiting to be questioned, and with always a vague reply in return.' [6] However, she was not as entirely dim as this description suggests, possessing 'a deep well of affection within her placid exterior'; like Fanny she remained fond of Rossetti to the end of his life.

The picture for which Alexa sat at Kelmscott was the green-and-orange *La Ghirlandata* (1873), and her admittedly rather vacant features, as perceived by the artist, can be seen in numerous similar images, among them the red-and-green *Regina Cordium* (1866), and the sumptuous golden *Monna Vanna* (1866) [103] as well as the later *Blessed Damozel* described earlier.

These are essentially decorative pieces, aesthetically composed and expressive of the glory of female beauty or femininity – of physical loveliness as perceived by the Pre-Raphaelite mind. In them is inscribed the glamour of the true 'stunner', whose moral and mental limitations are depicted in the lowness of her

brow; according to current popular phrenology, the highest intellectual faculties were ascribed to those with the highest foreheads, while the lower classes, Irish and 'savages' of all kinds were depicted as low-browed in relation to their supposed position in the evolutionary chain. Beautiful but brainless women – symbols of physical splendour without spiritual grace – were thus shown with compressed foreheads. The transitory nature of such allure was affirmed by the accessory flowers, whose temporary glory signifies the short life of feminine charms.

The shift in Pre-Raphaelite painting from the earlier moral and literary subjects to these abstract and symbolic meanings had a more elevated aspect too. It foreshadowed the development of aesthetics and the idea of 'art for art's sake', persuasively articulated in the essays of Walter Pater, responding to the ideas of Gautier and Baudelaire in France and Swinburne and Wilde in Britain. In his *Studies in the History of the Renaissance* (1873) Pater commended 'love of art for its own sake', rather than its moral import, as the only true wisdom. He asserted that the artist should burn 'with a hard, gem-like flame', and that 'all art aspires to the condition of music' – melodic, harmonious, but devoid of literal or paraphrasable meaning. The result in literature was the rhythmic, evocative, sonorous but ultimately absurd poetic style promoted by Swinburne and the Symbolists.

Allegorical subjects often came to be associated with individual women celebrated in the Pre-Raphaelite circle for their personality as well as looks, women whose appearance thereby took on an increasingly iconic role. Burne-Jones's sequence of *Seasons*, for example, with Maria Zambaco in diaphanous gown representing *Summer* (1869) [107] and the complementary image of Georgie in fur-wrapped mantle as *Winter* (1869) [106], is a striking example.

The meanings were not always so personal, and the device was used by women artists too, to convey elevated or abstract subjects that in some way relate to the models employed. Marie Spartali Stillman, the painter who also posed for Rossetti, Spencer Stanhope and Burne-Jones, was selected by Julia Margaret Cameron for various symbolic roles, as *The Spirit of the Vine* – perhaps in honour of her Greek ancestry – and as *Hypatia*, the renowned Alexandrian mathematician and philosopher martyred by Christian zealots and symbol of feminine learning. She also sat for Cameron's image of *Mnemosyne* (1868) [109], the pre-Olympian goddess of Memory, with long, loose hair and ivy tendrils.

106 (left) Edward Burne-Jones, Winter, *1869.*

107 (right) Edward Burne-Jones, Summer, *1869.*

Marie's admirers were united in her praise. 'She is so beautiful that I want to sit down and cry,' said Swinburne with characteristic extravagance. And her personality was equally attractive. 'I find her head about the most difficult I ever drew,' commented Rossetti, who used her for *A Vision of Fiametta* (1878) and for *The Bower Meadow* (1872), explaining 'It depends not nearly so much on real form as on subtle charm of life, which one cannot re-create'. [7]

Among Marie Spartali Stillman's own works were the watercolours *The Lady Prays – Desire* (1867), which was clearly inspired by Spenser's elaborate allegorical romance *The Faerie Queene*, and *Convent Lily* (1891) [108], a meditation on purity.

At the end of his career, Rossetti himself produced a canvas entitled *Mnemosyne* or *The Lamp of Memory* (1881), although the title betrays the rather random nature of his allegorization, since the image began life as an oil study for the monumental *Astarte Syriaca* [110], his tribute to the eternal female principle as embodied in the person of Jane Morris, whom the artist worshipped with the fervour of a devotee.

109 Julia Margaret Cameron,
Mnemosyne, *1868.*

108 (left) Marie Spartali Stillman,
Convent Lily, *1891.*

110 (right) Dante Gabriel Rossetti,
Astarte Syriaca, *1877.*

The story of Jane's later relationship with Rossetti is, however, a sad one;
in 1872 he suffered a schizophrenic collapse, after which he never fully
regained his sanity, and his life became dominated by paranoid delusions and
aural hallucinations. Although Jane looked after him devotedly at Kelmscott,
their relationship was permanently altered. 'That Gabriel *was* mad was but too
true', she wrote sadly after his death; 'no-one knows it better than myself.' [8]

She sat for the figure of *Astarte* over the winter of 1875–6, but then decided
that she could help him no further, and although remaining in affectionate
correspondence, thereafter ceased to see him except at occasional intervals.
Rossetti seems to have accepted this as inevitable; he continued to worship her
image and produced repeated versions of the same brooding, solitary female
figure, mysteriously powerful and melancholy.

112 (right) Dante Gabriel Rossetti, The Day
Dream, *1880.*

The statuesque *Astarte Syriaca*, larger than life-size and glowing with lurid
green and flesh tones, represents an ancient Syrian deity, older than Aphrodite
or Venus, symbolic of the Eternal Feminine; in the words of Rossetti's
accompanying sonnet:

> Torch-bearing, her sweet ministers compel
> All thrones of light beyond the sky and sea
> The witnesses of Beauty's face to be:
> That face, of Love's all-penetrative spell –
> Amulet, talisman and oracle –
> Betwixt the Sun and Moon a mystery.

The notion of mysterious, elemental womanhood was not Rossetti's invention,
but part of the general culture of the time. In such popular works as Rider
Haggard's *She*, published in 1887, she appears as a hidden all-powerful divine
being in the heart of Africa. Perhaps in response to this, Val Prinsep, who had
been the Pre-Raphaelites' young colleague for the Oxford murals, and was Julia
Margaret Cameron's nephew, produced a version of *Ayesha* – 'She Who Must
Be Obeyed'.

Rossetti's utter submission to Jane was gently and humorously satirized by
Burne-Jones in a little caricature of the 1870s, drawn for Maria Zambaco's
amusement, and showing the devoted, rotund artist carrying cushions for the
willowy and rather startled Jane [111]. This helps us to remember that the
sometimes strange notions of womanhood that flourished in the nineteenth
century were not necessarily based on actuality. In reality, Jane was far from
being or behaving like an icon to be worshipped; she was sensible, practical and
intelligent, with a witty and sensitive outlook on life. Dozens of pictures
portraying her features were produced by Rossetti, many completed from earlier
studies or photographs, such as the version of *Pandora* illustrated earlier [21].
Other titles included *Silence, Reverie, Aurea Catena, La Donna della Fiamma*, and
Perlascura. Most have no meaning beyond the metaphors suggested in the
titles, but testify to the artist's pictorial devotion to his sitter.

111 Edward Burne-Jones, Rossetti
Carrying Cushions for a Startled Janey
Morris, *c. 1870.*

113 Evelyn de Morgan, The Hour Glass, *1904–5.*

In *The Day Dream* of 1880 [112], Jane is shown in a green gown perched rather improbably in the branches of a young sycamore tree, whose unfurling leaf-buds convey the green vigour of spring and youth. On her knee is a book – we know that Jane was a voracious reader – and in her hand a honeysuckle flower which from other pictures seems to have represented sexual desire to Rossetti, with its pink and yellow tongue-like petals. The composition was derived from a drawing of Jane in a tree, done at Kelmscott in 1872, and probably originally contained a convolvulus motif. Jane herself favoured the snowdrop, St Agnes's flower, as the emblem here, but the tree's burgeoning leaves made this seasonally inappropriate, and finally Rossetti chose the honeysuckle. 'I think you look very like yourself now in the picture . . . seated full length with a dangling foot', he wrote nostalgically to Jane in 1880. [9] However, the image, which was also known as *Monna Primavera*, is not a portrait of Mrs Morris, nor even of the artist's mistress; it is a symbolic rendering of spring, personified, in the words of the accompanying sonnet, as 'woman's budding day-dream spirit-fanned', while the 'embowered throstle's urgent woodnotes soar Through summer silence . . .'. In the dense green and swirling foliage of the canvas, Jane is transformed into the spirit of Nature.

The spirit of Music is the subject of Kate Bunce's evocation of *Melody (Musica)* [115] with her lute, and painted in a harmony of reds and greens.

In her old age, Jane was chosen by the young painter Evelyn de Morgan – wife of the ceramic artist William de Morgan and friend of the Morris family – to sit for a symbolic portrayal of the passing of time, in *The Hour Glass* (1904–5) [113]. The relation of this solemn figure to its study [114], recognizable as a portrait of an individual in a way the finished work is not, indicates how female features were transformed, in this type of painting, from personal to abstract concepts. Perhaps, too, the picture carries a hint of personality, an oblique allusion to Jane's lifelong love of music and her reputation as an embroiderer. According to the artist, who specialized in works of intense and opaque symbolism, the picture is 'an echo of a movement in the Waldstein Sonata of Beethoven'. In the doorway Eternal Life stands piping, 'but the seated woman is thinking only of the Sands of Life running out in the Hour Glass at her side. The figures in the tapestry behind her are symbolic of the past joys of life.' [10] Thus, although *The Hour Glass* is not a picture of Jane, it shows how, by the end of the century, her face had attained iconic meaning, usable by others as well as Rossetti for the expression of abstract and allegorical ideas. And does the reference to Eternal Life indicate, perhaps, the immortality conferred on the model by the representations of art? In this images, Jane and the other Pre-Raphaelite women attain a kind of eternal, abiding presence.

114 Evelyn de Morgan, study of the head of Jane Morris in old age for the painting The Hour Glass, *c. 1904.*

115 (right) Kate Elizabeth Bunce, Melody (Musica), *date unknown.*

Pale Ladies of Death

Death, love and sex were powerfully if invisibly linked in Victorian culture and, as the century progressed, painters and poets made the link increasingly, even sensationally, explicit. By the 1890s, the Decadent writer Arthur Symons was echoing Swinburne in his praise of death:

> O pale and heavy-lidded woman, why is your cheek
> Pale as the dead, and what are your eyes afraid lest they speak?
> And the woman answered me: I am pale as the dead
> For the dead have loved me, and I dream of the dead . . .

In 'The Garden of Proserpine', Swinburne rhapsodized on the mythical bride of Pluto, in the world of the afterlife: 'Pale, beyond porch and portal, Crowned with calm leaves . . .'. Death-like, she has languid lips and 'cold immortal hands'.

At the start of the Pre-Raphaelite age, the artistic imagery of death was largely sentimental, its pathos expressive of the simple griefs of loss and regret. With the strength of romantic love and the frequency of youthful mortality, a broken, grieving heart was the conventional figure for odes to the beloved in death. Characteristically, Christina Rossetti's deceptively simple 'Song' takes issue with sentimentality, while conveying the true sadness of loss:

> When I am dead, my dearest,
> Sing no sad songs for me;
> Plant thou no roses at my head
> Nor shady cypress tree.
>
> Be the green grass over me
> With showers and dewdrops wet,
> And if thou wilt, remember,
> And if thou wilt, forget.

116 Dante Gabriel Rossetti, Beata Beatrix, c. *1864–70.*

117 *John Everett Millais,* Ophelia, *1852.*

To represent sorrowful, pathetic death, the Pre-Raphaelite painters took the character of Ophelia, Shakespeare's heroine who, rejected by Hamlet, becomes insane and drowns, dying of a broken heart. Millais's celebrated version of *Ophelia* (1852) [117] shows her floating down a lovely, flower-strewn stream, singing in her madness, oblivious of tragedy. It was among the earliest depictions of the theme and keeps faithfully to Shakespeare's text; today it retains its impact through the strange disjunction of image and content: the bright flowers and foliage of spring are at odds with the drowning girl.

The context of this painting later became almost as famous as the canvas itself, which must be the best-known of all Pre-Raphaelite paintings. The riverbank was painted first, on site – according to early Pre-Raphaelite principles of truth to nature and *plein-air* painting – by the Hogsmill stream in Surrey. The figure of Ophelia, however, was painted in the studio during the winter months from Elizabeth Siddal, still at this date working as a model. She posed wearing an antique brocade gown, 'all flowered over with silver embroidery', in a tin bath-tub filled with water, kept warm with small candles underneath. Millais painted with such concentration, according to Arthur Hughes, that on one occasion the candles were allowed to go out, and by the time Lizzie was rescued from the water she was numb with cold and nearly caught pneumonia – an ominous prefiguring of her own death.

The flowers floating with Ophelia are emblematic of her fate: pansies, signifying thought and vain love; a necklace of violets, symbolizing faithful chastity and the death of the young; a poppy, death's flower; and forget-me-nots, their meaning contained in their name.

In the same year, Arthur Hughes produced his own version of *Ophelia* [118] showing a pubescent girl, with green rushes in her hair, distractedly dropping petals into a stagnant pool. This portrays the moment before Ophelia, leaning out on a willow branch, falls 'into the weeping brook'. Unlike Millais's jocund landscape, Hughes's setting evokes a spooky atmosphere of apprehension, conveyed by the unnatural light on the figure, whose emaciated form is suggestive of insanity, and by the inclusion of a bat, gliding ominously through the gloom.

Rossetti was also drawn to the story of sad Ophelia, depicting at least three moments from the play in sketches and drawings, the most significant of which is an intricate ink composition showing *Ophelia returning Hamlet's Betrothal Gifts* (1859) at the moment of his cruel rejection, with the words inscribed on the frame: 'I loved you not . . . Get thee to a nunnery'.

In the Victorian age, a woman rejected by her lover was a sad figure. Conventional wisdom decreed that her chances of marriage were slim: other men did not look for second-hand or 'reject' merchandise. And the notion of everlasting romantic love meant that the jilted girl, symbolically at least, was expected to remain faithful to her beloved; unrequited passion was no less

118 Arthur Hughes, Ophelia, *1852.*

eternal. In art, death by drowning or decline were appropriate endings for rejected women.

There was bitter irony in Rossetti's choice of this scene from *Hamlet*, for in 1858 he apparently broke off his unofficial engagement to Lizzie while the couple were staying in Derbyshire, and returned to London fancy free. Lizzie vanished from view; there are no contemporary references to her in Pre-Raphaelite sources until 1860, when she reappeared on the scene, now seriously ill. It seems likely that during this estrangement, which was expected to be permanent, she wrote the sad and angry verses that, like Christina's, anticipate death and regret. Parts of her poem 'A Year and a Day' seem to evoke the atmosphere of *Ophelia*:

> I lie among the tall green grass
>   That bends above my head
> And covers up my wasted face
>   And folds me in its bed
> Tenderly and lovingly
>   Like grass above the dead.
>
> The river ever running down
>   Between its grassy bed
> The voices of a thousand birds
>   That clang above my head
> Shall bring to me a sadder dream
>   When this sad dream is dead.

Towards the end of the century, J. W. Waterhouse produced no less than three pictures of Ophelia, as if obsessed with this Pre-Raphaelite theme. In the earliest, painted in 1889, *Ophelia* is lying in a riverside meadow in an attitude of deranged abandon, one hand in her tousled hair, the other grasping flowers. Although the water is only glimpsed in the background, the horizontal composition and spring foliage recall Millais's famous image, which was shown in public at the 1872 International Exhibition in London.

Waterhouse's second version of *Ophelia (1894)* is closer to Hughes's interpretation, showing Ophelia by the side of a similar gnarled willow tree overhanging the water. 'Ophelia sits by the margin of a lily-strewn pool' ran the description of Waterhouse's canvas in the New Gallery's catalogue. 'Her lank auburn tresses, decked with daisies and poppies, stream down her back. She wears a silvery-grey costume, gold-embroidered and bejewelled, with a golden baldric.'[1] The third Waterhouse version, *Ophelia*, painted in 1910, is the best-known; it shows a staring-eyed, full-bosomed woman in blue silk gown, clutching a handful of flowers – an arresting image, distinctively Pre-Raphaelite in feeling if not, strictly speaking, in terms of technique.

Waterhouse's models – virtually all female – have proved difficult to identify despite their regular appearance on canvas. However, it is clear that female models were as essential to his inspiration as they were to that of the earlier Pre-Raphaelite painters:

> The paintings show how as the years went by he continually sought his ideal vision of womanhood . . . and remained faithful to her in his art, reflecting the distant ideal of courtly love in the warmed mirrors of Italian passion and Greek sensuality.[2]

For Ophelia, the mirrors were cool, watery and English, in homage to her Pre-Raphaelite origins.

Another literary character identified with death – and also with Elizabeth Siddal – is of course Dante's beloved Beatrice, as refracted through Rossetti's imagination. The painter's close knowledge of and association with the poet – owing to his Italian father's obsession with the cabbalistic significance of the texts, Gabriel was given Dante as a middle name, which he later moved to first position, always signing himself 'D.G.R.' – gave the idea of the unattainable Beatrice a special significance in his art, as an image both of the perfect woman and of the artist's unattainable ideal.

Among the earliest works for which Lizzie sat was the small watercolour of *Beatrice Denying her Salutation* (1851–2). She appeared again, as an attendant lady in *Dante Drawing an Angel on the Anniversary of Beatrice's Death* (1853), and as the beloved herself in the small watercolour version of *Dante's Dream at the Time of the Death of Beatrice* (1856), where Beatrice and Death are linked by Love as she lies on her bier.

When, to the surprise of family and friends, Lizzie reappeared in the spring of 1860, with Rossetti making urgent plans for marriage, she was gravely ill and, he believed, on the verge of death; his guilt-induced promise of marriage was designed to save her life. It is likely that her illness was near-fatal drug addiction, for she had contracted the habit of taking large quantities of the tincture of opium known as laudanum, freely available in the Victorian age and used to dull the pain of both disease and distress. Lizzie survived, and was married to Rossetti, but during their honeymoon in Paris his anxiety and foreboding expressed itself in an intense, macabre drawing called *How They Met Themselves* (1851–60) [119], showing a pair of young lovers, modelled on himself and Lizzie, meeting their doubles in a dark forest – a *doppelgänger* encounter symbolic of impending death, and an ominous nuptial image. On their return to London, Lizzie became pregnant, but the child was stillborn. She grew depressed, disturbed and was still deeply addicted to the drug. In February 1862 she died of an overdose of laudanum, self-administered either deliberately or with careless disregard of the danger.

Rossetti's painting of *Beata Beatrix* [116], inspired by Dante's *Vita Nuova* and portraying the beloved at the moment of her transition from earth to heaven, was the artist's mourning tribute to his wife; it shows Lizzie in a pose very similar to that of the early drawings of her for *Delia*, with eyes closed in ecstatic expectation. In the artist's words, it is an ideal image of death, symbolized by 'sudden spiritual transformation. Beatrice is rapt visibly into heaven seeing as it were through her shut lids'. The 'radiant bird, a messenger of death' drops a poppy into her hands. In the background Dante, the lover, gazes towards Love 'in whose hand the waning life of his lady flickers as a flame. On the sundial at her side the shadow falls on the hour of nine . . .'. [3]

---

119 *Dante Gabriel Rossetti,* How They Met Themselves 1851–60, *1860.*

The first version of *Beata Beatrix* was begun around 1864 and completed in 1870. A replica, complete with predella showing Dante's meeting with Beatrice in paradise, was painted in 1871–2 for the patron William Graham. This was the period of Rossetti's mental breakdown, triggered by the hostile response to his *Poems* (1870), a volume which, although largely inspired by the artist's new adoration of Janey, also included poems from a manuscript notebook buried in Lizzie's coffin in 1862 as an expression of remorse, and exhumed seven years later. The volume therefore represented a double betrayal, of Lizzie's love and of her grave. *Beata Beatrix* has always been interpreted as a strong if somewhat sentimental token of the artist's grief and guilt, and his return to the identical subject in the creation of a replica suggests some kind of desperate desire to make amends. It is, however, also a truly macabre image, of the beloved woman at the moment of death, painted in the sensuous style of Rossetti's middle period, and its sense of necrophiliac longing is hard to evade.

Many years later, a small picture of Lizzie [120], showing her wrapped in a matronly shawl, came to light in romantic circumstances. Around 1905, a lady engaged in charitable visiting in London's East End saw it in the room of an elderly widow, who identified it as the portrait 'of the wife of a painter man', who had died young. The midwife who attended Lizzie's tragic confinement, according to the source, 'begged to have some memento. The painter man gave her this; it is only a coloured photo'. [4] And so indeed it proved, although the picture was sold as a genuine miniature by Rossetti to the collector J. Pierpont Morgan, who added the jewelled Fabergé frame. The money was used to purchase an annuity for the old woman and keep her from the degradation of the workhouse infirmary.

This touching tale of a posthumous portrait, painted by Rossetti onto one of the few surviving photographic images of Lizzie, together with the visual similarities with the closed eyes and clasped hands of Beatrice, suggest a possible relation between photo and painting, despite the immense difference of scale and purpose.

120 *Dante Gabriel Rossetti (overpainting on photograph)*, Elizabeth Rossetti, *c. 1861.*

Grief and mourning for the loss of a wife were the stimulus for Holman Hunt's return, in the later 1860s, to the story of Isabella with which the PRB began. Following his failure with Annie and his rejection by Julia Jackson, Hunt proposed to Fanny Waugh, to whom he was married in December 1865 [122]. The couple at once set off for the Middle East, where Hunt hoped to resume the painting of the biblical scenes for which he had become renowned, but they were delayed by cholera in Italy, where, tragically, Fanny died from puerperal fever following the birth of her son.

Perhaps prophetically, the enforced stay in Florence had given Hunt the idea of 'a delicious subject' based on his old source of inspiration, also set in Italy, and showing *Isabella and the Pot of Basil* (1867) [121] with the heroine mourning her beloved Lorenzo, whose head is gruesomely hidden in the plant pot. Perhaps Hunt also realized, following the success of *The Afterglow in Egypt* and *Il Dolce*

121 (left) William Holman Hunt,
Isabella and the Pot of Basil, *1867.*

122 William Holman Hunt
Fanny Holman Hunt, *1866–8.*

123 *Dante Gabriel Rossetti,* Proserpine, *1873–7.*

Far Niente, not to mention Rossetti's numerous carnal visions, that life-size figures in romantic guise were equally if not more saleable than biblical scenes.

With Fanny's death, however, *Isabella* became 'not only a celebration of the love Hunt had experienced during his year-long marriage, in the sensuality of the figure' – in her near-transparent shift – 'but also an expression of the anguish of his bereavement'. [5] The artist himself wrote to a friend: 'Tho' all day long my mind has a burden of grief singing thro' it, I can direct it to work . . . and this with less difficulty because she for whom I suffer – sat at my side – while I planned the task I am doing . . .'. [6]

Isabella has created a shrine for her basil pot, on an inlaid prie-dieu with an embroidered cloth bearing his name. Hunt himself designed and painted the majolica pot over which Isabella's disordered tresses flow; the death's-head motif on the handle and other details are emblems of the convergence of love and loss. Inconsolable, Isabella is dying of grief. Ten years later Holman Hunt married Fanny's younger sister Edith.

Other pining figures representing death and love were depicted by Rossetti as tokens of his love for Jane and expressive of his despair. Since she was married to someone else, and divorce was impossible, their love for each other could find expression only through adultery or fantasy – and the pictures were in my view created from this sense of desperate but romantic impossibility. The most powerful image is that of *Proserpine* [123], hymned by Swinburne as a metaphor of beloved death and pagan joy, and shown by Rossetti as a creature of winter, the death of natural growth, and darkness. Proserpine is captive in the underworld, because she has eaten pomegranate seeds, shown here in carnal red. 'She is represented in a gloomy corridor of her palace, with the fatal fruit in her hand', the artist explained to a client. 'As she passes, a gleam strikes on the wall behind her, admitting for a moment the light of the upper world . . . The ivy branch in the background may be taken as a symbol of clinging memory.' [7]

Proserpine is of course bound to her hated husband Pluto for only half the year, and the subject would appear to have unmistakable personal reference to Rossetti's perception of the winter months his beloved Jane spent in London with her husband William Morris. Kelmscott Manor, where Jane and Rossetti were together and where *Proserpine* was largely painted, was a summer residence only, on account of winter damp and floods. Several versions of the subject were painted, as if Rossetti could not leave the theme alone.

A similar subject is presented in *La Pia de' Tolomei* (1868–80) [124], which also depicts Jane's brooding face and long mobile fingers. The story is derived from Dante, and portrays poor Pia, imprisoned by a cruel husband in a fortress where she dies of despair and disease. 'The lady reclines on the ramparts', explained Fred Stephens, 'her thumb and forefinger clasp tightly, even to the whitening of nail and knuckle, the "fair jewel" on the other . . . On her features are no signs of animation, or hope, or care for existence . . .' [8] The 'fair jewel' is her wedding

124 *Dante Gabriel Rossetti*, La Pia de' Tolomei,
1868–80.

ring, the tragic symbol of her imprisonment and decline.

The most popular Victorian lady of death was probably Tennyson's Elaine, whose *Idyll* represents the tragic face of true love:

> Elaine the fair, Elaine the loveable,
> Elaine the lily maid of Astolat,
> High in her chamber up a tower to the east
> Guarded the sacred shield of Lancelot.

Having fallen in love with the gallant knight without knowing his identity, and unable to alter her feelings when she learns of his unavailability, Elaine is doomed to romantic frustration, everlastingly faithful to unrequited love. She sings 'The Song of Love and Death', in which the two are interchangeable:

Love, art thou sweet? Then bitter death must be:
Love, thou art bitter, sweet is death to me.
O love, if death be sweeter, let me die.

Like Ophelia, Elaine loses her wits and floats down the river to Camelot, on her final 'dolorous voyage':

I fain would follow death, if that could be;
I needs must follow death, who calls for me;
Call and I follow, I follow! Let me die.

Julia Margaret Cameron, in her determined efforts to illustrate the Poet Laureate's works, produced two images of Elaine. The first, entitled *Call, I follow, I follow – let me die* (1867) [125], is a simple dramatic image of a woman's head in profile. It was published by the Autotype Company – which later made reproductions of Rossetti's works – during the time that *Beata Beatrix* was on the easel, and has been identified as an influence on the soft background imagery and haloed, top-lit figure, although it is clear that the poetic nature of Rossetti's paintings was an equally powerful influence on Cameron's photographic style.

In 1874 Cameron produced *Elaine the Lily Maid of Astolat*, a more literal image, showing the heroine tending Lancelot's shield, for which she has embroidered a case and with which she sits daydreaming of imagined heroic adventures.

When Gustave Doré illustrated *Elaine* for the Moxon edition of Tennyson's *Idylls* in 1868, he showed her on her last river journey, drifting through a Romantic landscape, and a similar image was chosen by J. Atkinson Grimshaw for his second version of *Elaine* (1877), with green and gold obsequies, where the funeral barge is a black gondola with a dragon prow and a sinister boatman, the tongueless servant of the poem. Together they glide silently to Camelot, a sacrificial offering to Lancelot:

In her right hand the lily, in her left
The letter – all her bright hair streaming down –
And all the coverlid was cloth of gold
Drawn to her waist, and she herself in white
All but her face, and that clear featur'd face
Was lovely, for she did not seem as dead,
But fast asleep, and lay as though she smil'd.

Embalmed in death, the beautiful pale woman remains desirable and, as it were, still willing, a strange and compelling image of love, sex and loss.

125 *Julia Margaret Cameron,*
Call, I follow, I follow – let me die, *1867.*

Conclusion

The other legendary Pre-Raphaelite heroine who floated down the river to Camelot was of course the Lady of Shalott – who indeed shared the same medieval ancestry as Elaine, 'Shalott' and 'Astolat' being alternative versions of the same name – and whose tale inspired repeated pictorial images. In 1985 an exhibition in the United States was devoted entirely to Victorian 'Ladies of Shalott', their sources and context.

In Tennyson's poem, with its hypnotic rhythm and repetition, the lady is imprisoned on an island, forbidden to look directly at the world, watching only through a mirror whose reflections she weaves into a tapestry web. Solitary and mysteriously accursed, she dreams of her own 'loyal knight', and confesses herself 'half sick of shadows', yearning for real experience. So when the shining image of Lancelot, the red cross knight, appears in her mirror, she suddenly breaks the ban:

> She left the web, she left the loom,
> She made three paces through the room,
> She saw the water-lily bloom,
> She saw the helmet and the plume,
>   She looked down to Camelot.
> Out flew the web and floated wide,
> The mirror crack'd from side to side:
> 'The curse is come upon me,' cried
>   The Lady of Shalott.

Among the earliest representations was a *Lady of Shalott* drawn by Elizabeth Siddal at the start of her artistic career in 1853. In this the lady is shown, with characteristic early Pre-Raphaelite awkwardness, seated at her loom, turning fatefully to look through the window at Lancelot.

Most artists chose to depict this moment, the most dramatic in the poem, when the lady is condemned to die. She leaves her tower, finds a boat and drifts down river, singing as she dies. Lancelot is among those who watch as she arrives, saying: 'She has a lovely face; God in his mercy send her grace.'

Holman Hunt depicted the moment of disobedience firstly in 1850, and secondly in 1857, with a detailed image for engraving in the Moxon Tennyson [127]. For the same volume Rossetti produced an image from the end of the poem, showing Lancelot gazing at the lady.

126 John William Waterhouse, 'I am Half Sick of Shadows' said the Lady of Shalott, *1915.*

In 1854 Millais showed her floating downriver, and in 1858 William Maw Egley painted a High Gothick version full of antiquarian detail, a relatively early example of the influence of Pre-Raphaelite medievalism on other artists [128]; one contemporary critic called it an 'ill-favoured specimen . . . of flagrant Pre-Raphaelitism', but modern scholars take issue rather with its antiquarian accumulation of stage props in place of the poetic intensity of the PRB style, and with the authentic fourteenth-century costume, which 'clothes somewhat incongruously the patently Victorian figure of Mrs Egley, who was the model.'[1] But the claustrophobic atmosphere of the painting is fully expressive of the text.

In 1861 Henry Peach Robinson produced a now-famous photographic reconstruction of the Lady of Shalott, created according to Pre-Raphaelite principles. 'I made a barge,' he wrote later, 'crimped the model's hair, Pre-Raphaelite fashion, laid her on the boat in the river among the water-lilies, and gave her a background of weeping willows, taken in the rain so that they might look dreary.' [2]

In the last quarter of the century, Holman Hunt returned to the subject, in what has been called his 'last and greatest' Pre-Raphaelite picture, based on his earlier illustration. This shows the lady entangled in her web, her hair floating wildly about her head, on a very large canvas crowded with exotic decorative detail. This glows with dramatic colour within a dense pattern of encircling lines.

True to form, the prolific J. W. Waterhouse produced three separate versions of the story, using his favourite dark-haired model, and showing her firstly, in the *Lady of Shalott* (1888), casting off her boat in what looks like an overgrown backwater of the Thames, her tapestry web trailing in the water. The second *Lady of Shalott* (1894) shows her entangled in threads in a manner similar to Hunt's composition, while the third version *'I am Half Sick of Shadows' said the Lady of Shalott* (1915) [126] shows her at an elaborate loom, gazing languorously at the mirrored sight of young lovers and Camelot in the distance. A very similar moment is also presented in S. H. Meteyard's picture of the same title dated 1913.

Several dozen other depictions of the Lady of Shalott might be cited, but the striking aspect of those ladies illustrated here is their powerful imagery of confinement and bondage, presaged by the poem in its tale of solitary seclusion, but strongly emphasized by the artists. The bondage motif evidently presented itself to the painters despite Tennyson's own claim that the poem articulated the dilemma of art, caught between reflection and reality or, alternatively, a metaphor of the sudden transformation through the power of love from the world of shadows to that of substance. On his own account, Holman Hunt analysed the text as a moral fable illustrating 'the failure of a human soul towards its accepted responsibility'. [3] In the poem, the prohibition on the lady is arbitrary, but in Hunt's picture the iconography is of moral disobedience and the conflict between good and evil.

127 *William Holman Hunt*, The Lady of Shalott, *1857.*

128 William Maw Egley, The Lady of Shalott, *1858.*

Nevertheless, it is hard to read his, or the other, images as anything but an oblique account of the confined and restricted world of the Victorian woman – accursed and prohibited by virtue of her sex alone – and the dire consequences attendant on rebellion. The rejection of seclusion in the shadowy sphere of prescribed femininity, where the approved activity is weaving or embroidery, leads immediately to ostracism and social death. The enclosed rooms in which these ladies live, looking out on inviting sunlit landscapes, and the tangled strands binding their vigorous limbs, are surely metaphors of woman's condition, signifying the docile, passive, reflective and domestic role that dominated Victorian ideas of femininity. The lady cannot break free from her constraints: her gesture of independence provokes the curse. It is interesting that most artists chose to depict this particular moment, so that their ladies are frozen forever in their decision of defiance.

A similar message seems to be submerged in Evelyn de Morgan's disturbing painting *The Captives* [129], which shows five nubile maidens in flowing drapery assailed by mythical monsters, in a moment of permanent tension: they neither escape nor submit.

As a student at the Slade School of Art in London in the 1870s, Evelyn de Morgan had been angry and rebellious at the social restrictions imposed on women, especially those that decreed that art was an accomplishment rather than a serious commitment for women, and the middle-class convention that young ladies should never go out unaccompanied. On her journeys to and from the Slade, Evelyn tried stubbornly to evade the servant assigned to her as escort. When forbidden to paint, she continued to work secretly in her room.

The shadowy dragons in *The Captives* have been interpreted as the frightening phantoms of the maidens' own creation, the terrors and fears of the mind's imagining. They are not to be given a single definitive analysis, however, since their meaning is open, and can equally be read as representing the oppression of the outer world, the fearsome demons of patriarchy, whose chief victims are young women. Although oppressive, they are shadowy, existing only in the realm of ideas.

A comparable theme is handled more explicitly in de Morgan's *The Gilded Cage* [130], the artist's last work before her death in 1919. This shows a restless and discontented young woman, married to an elderly husband, looking enviously out of the window at a group of gypsy figures dancing in the open air. A wild bird soars freely, contrasting with the one in a gilded cage, symbolic of the woman's own fate. This is more than a simple allegory of youth and age, notwithstanding the personal reference to Evelyn's own much older husband; this is captive femininity, confined by old ideas, and longing for freedom.

It is an appropriate image to conclude this study of so many representations of women, real and imaginary, confined within the gilded cage of the Pre-Raphaelite picture frame.

129 Evelyn de Morgan, The Captives, *c. 1888.*

130 Evelyn de Morgan, The Gilded Cage, *1919.*

Notes and References

Introduction

1   Henry Cotton, *Indian and Home Memories*, 1911, p. 53.
2   Martin Harrison and Bill Waters, *Burne-Jones*, 1979, p. 66.
3   William Holman Hunt, *Pre-Raphaelitism and the Pre-Raphaelite Brotherhood*, 1905, I, p. 87.

8   Malcolm Warner, *The Pre-Raphaelites*, Tate Gallery exhibition catalogue, 1984, p. 26.
9   Susan Casteras, 'Virgin Vows', *Victorian Studies*, 24, p. 178.
10 D. G. Rossetti to Fanny Cornforth, in Baum, op. cit., p. 5.
11. Phyllis Rose, *Woman of Letters: A Life of Virginia Woolf*, 1978, p. 10.

Bohemians and Stunners

1   J. G. Millais, *John Everett Millais*, 1899. I, p. 149.
2   Virginia Surtees, *The Paintings and Drawings of Dante Gabriel Rossetti: A Catalogue Raisonné*, 1971, I, p. 222, n. 1.
3   Joseph Knight, *Dante Gabriel Rossetti*, 1887, p. 70.
4   D. G. Rossetti to W. Bell Scott, quoted in Andrea Rose, *Pre-Raphaelite Portraits*, 1981, p. 102.
5   D. G. Rossetti to Ellen Heaton, 25 October 1863, quoted in Surtees, op. cit., p. 92, n. 7.
6   D. G. Rossetti to Fanny Cornforth, September 1873, printed in *The Letters of D. G Rossetti to Fanny Cornforth*, ed. P. Baum, 1940, p. 61.
7   Entry for 13 April 1863, *The Diaries of George Price Boyce*, ed. V. Surtees, 1980, p. 45.

Holy Virgins

1   D. G. Rossetti to F. G. Stephens, 8 September 1852, quoted by Alastair Grieve, in *The Pre-Raphaelites*, Tate Gallery exhibition catalogue, 1984, p. 65.
2   D. G. Rossetti to Charles Lyell, 14 November 1848, quoted in Alastair Grieve, *The Art of D. G. Rossetti: The Pre-Raphaelite Period*, 1973, p. 7.
3   A. Grieve, Tate Gallery exhibition catalogue, 1984, p. 65.
4   W. Holman Hunt, op. cit., I, p. 29.
5   Susan Casteras, *The Substance or the Shadow*, 1982, p. 67.
6   Martha Vicinus, *Independent Women 1850–1920*, 1985, p. 47.
7   Alastair Grieve, 'Illustrations to *The Saint's Tragedy* by three Pre-Raphaelite Artists', *Burlington Magazine*, 1969, p. 293.

Nubile Maidens

1   Judith Bronkhurst, Tate Gallery exhibition catalogue, 1984, p. 245.
2   See Malcolm Warner, 'John Everett Millais's *Autumn Leaves*', Pre-Raphaelite Papers, 1984, pp. 126ff.
3   F. G. Stephens, *Athenaeum*, 8 May 1880.
4   John Ruskin to Ellen Heaton, quoted in Surtees, op. cit., p. 37.

Doves and Mothers

1   Ford Madox Brown, 1865 Descriptive Catalogue, quoted by Mary Bennett, Tate Gallery exhibition catalogue, 1984, p. 124.
2   Ibid.
3   See Elaine Shefer, 'Deverell, Rossetti, Siddal and "The Bird in the Cage"', *Art Bulletin*, LXVII, 3, September 1985, pp. 437–47.
4   John Everett Millais to W. Holman Hunt quoted in Mary Lutyens, *Millais and the Ruskins*, 1967, n. p. 150.
5   John Ruskin to Ellen Heaton, November 1855, quoted in Virginia Surtees, *Sublime and Instructive*, 1972, p. 177.
6   John Ruskin, 'Of Queens' Gardens', *Sesame and Lilies*, 1865, pp. 97–8.
7   Quoted by Mary Bennett, Tate Gallery exhibition catalogue, 1984, p. 240.
08 Entry for 8 July 1855, *The Diary of Ford Madox Brown*, ed. Virginia Surtees, 1981, p. 142.
9   H. Wilson, *The Artist*, 1897, quoted by Mary Bennett, Tate Gallery exhibition catalogue, 1984, p. 150.
10 John Ruskin to Georgiana Burne-Jones, 22 November 1861, in *The Collected Works of John Ruskin*, 1912, Letters, I, pp. 393–4.
11 John Ruskin, Preface to *Sesame and Lilies*, 1871 edn, p. xxxiv.

Fallen Magdalens

1 John Ruskin in *The Times* 24 May 1854, quoted by Judith Bronkhurst, Tate Gallery exhibition catalogue, 1984, p. 121.
2 D. G. Rossetti to W. Holman Hunt, 30 January 1855, quoted by Alastair Grieve, Tate Gallery exhibition catalogue, 1984, p. 265.
3 Fanny Cornforth, quoted in Baum, op. cit., p. 4.
4 A. C. Swinburne to W. Bell Scott, 16 December 1859, *Swinburne Letters*, ed. C. Y. Lang, 1959, I, p. 27.
5 W. Holman Hunt to Thomas Combe, 12 February 1860, Bodleian Library MSS. Eng. lett. c. 296.
6 Jeannette Marshall's Diary, quoted in Zuzanna Shonfield, *The Precariously Privileged*, 1987, p. 112.
7 Frederic Shields, quoted in Ernestine Mills, *The Life and Letters of Frederic Shields 1833–1911*, 1912, p. 282.

Medieval Damozels

1 J. G. Millais, op. cit., II, p. 24.

Sorceresses

1 Edward Burne-Jones to H. M. Gaskell, January 1893, quoted in Penelope Fitzgerald, *Edward Burne-Jones*, 1975, p. 127.
2 Ibid., p. 150.
3 *The Collected Works of John Ruskin*, 1912, XVII, p. 213.
4 Edward Burne-Jones quoted in Fitzgerald, op. cit., p. 115.
5 See John Christian, Tate Gallery exhibition catalogue, 1984, pp. 229–31.
6 Anthony Hobson, *J. W. Waterhouse*, 1980, p. 76.

Allegories and Icons

1 Marina Warner, *Monuments and Maidens*, 1985, p. 331.
2 W. Holman Hunt to Thomas Combe, 27 April 1854, quoted by Judith Bronkhurst, Tate Gallery exhibition catalogue, 1984, p. 162.
3 W. Holman Hunt to Edward Lear, 10 September 1862, John Rylands Library, Manchester, quoted by Bronkhurst, Tate Gallery exhibition catalogue, 1984, p. 162.

4 W. Holman Hunt to Ernest Chesneau, 3 December 1882, quoted by Bronkhurst, Tate Gallery exhibition catalogue, 1984, p. 163.
5 Edward Burne-Jones to H. M. Gaskell, January 1893, quoted in Fitzgerald, *Edward Burne-Jones*, p. 82.
6 H. Treffry Dunn, quoted in Andrea Rose, *Pre-Raphaelite Portraits*, 1981, p. 109.
7 D. G. Rossetti to Jane Morris, 14 August 1869, British Library MSS Add. 52332.
8 Jane Morris to T. Watts-Dunton, 1883, British Library MSS Add. 45353.
9 D. G. Rossetti to Jane Morris, February 1880, British Library MSS Add. 52332.
10 Catalogue of the pictures, *Cragside*, National Trust, 1985, p. 48.

Pale Ladies of Death

1 Catalogue of New Gallery, London 1894, quoted by A. Hobson, *J. W. Waterhouse*, 1980, p. 186, where the description is mistakenly confused with another picture with the same title, dated 1910, but reproduced by Hobson as pl. 165. The account of Ophelia as *seated* and dressed in a silver-grey gown in the 1894 catalogue indicates that the picture of this date is not the blue-gowned standing figure illustrated by Hobson.
2 A. Hobson, *J. W. Waterhouse*, 1980, p. 171
3 D. G. Rossetti to William Graham, 11 March 1873, quoted by A. Grieve, Tate Gallery exhibition catalogue, 1984, p. 209.
4 G. C. Williamson, *Country Life*, 11 July 1936.
5 Judith Bronkhurst, Tate Gallery exhibition catalogue, 1984, p. 216.
6 W. Holman Hunt to Thomas Combe, 1 February 1867, John Rylands Library, Manchester, quoted by Bronkhurst, Tate Gallery exhibition catalogue, 1984, p. 216.
7 D. G. Rossetti to W. A. Turner, quoted by William Sharp, *Dante Gabriel Rossetti*, 1882, p. 236.
8 F. G. Stephens, *Athenaeum*, 26 February 1881.

Conclusion

1 See *William Morris and the Middle Ages*, ed. J. Banham and J. Harris, Manchester 1984, p. 168.
2 H. P. Robinson, *Photographic Quarterly*, 1892, quoted in Arts Council, *Masterpieces of Victorian Photography 1840–1900*, 1951, pp. 21–2.
3 W. Holman Hunt, *PreRaphaelitism and the Pre-Raphaelite Brotherhood*, 1905, II, p. 401.

List of Illustrations

64 Joanna Mary Wells (née Boyce), *Gretchen*, 1861. Oil, 72.4 × 43.2 cm ($28\frac{1}{2}$ × 17 in). Tate Gallery, London.

65 William Holman Hunt, *The Hireling Shepherd*, 1851. Oil on canvas, 76.4 × 109.5 cm ($30\frac{1}{16}$ × $43\frac{1}{8}$ in). City of Manchester Art Galleries.

66 Unknown photographer, *Annie Miller*, *c.* 1860. Photograph. Private Collection.

67 William Holman Hunt, *The Awakening Conscience*, 1853. Oil on canvas, 76.2 × 55.9 cm (30 × 22 in). Tate Gallery, London.

68 Dante Gabriel Rossetti, *Found* (detail), 1854–81. Oil on canvas, 91.4 × 80 cm (36 × $31\frac{1}{2}$ in). Delaware Art Museum, Samuel and Mary R. Bancroft Memorial Collection.

69 Dante Gabriel Rossetti, study for *Found*, 1858. Ink, 17.7 × 19.6 cm (7 × $7\frac{3}{4}$ in). By courtesy of Birmingham Museums and Art Gallery.

70 W. and D. Downey, *Fanny Cornforth*, 1863. Photograph. Jeremy Maas (photo: National Portrait Gallery).

71 Dante Gabriel Rossetti, *Blue Bower*, 1865. Oil on canvas, 84 × 70.9 cm ($33\frac{1}{16}$ × $27\frac{7}{8}$ in). The Barber Institute of Fine Arts, The University of Birmingham.

72 Dante Gabriel Rossetti, *Bocca Baciata*, 1860. Oil on panel, 33.7 × 30.5 cm ($13\frac{1}{4}$ × 12 in). Courtesy, Museum of Fine Arts, Boston: Gift of James Lawrence.

73 Dante Gabriel Rossetti, *Mary Magdalene at the Door of Simon the Pharisee*, 1858. Pen and ink on paper, 52.7 × 45.7 cm ($20\frac{3}{4}$ × 18 in). Fitzwilliam Museum, Cambridge.

74 Anthony Frederick Sandys, illustration for *If*, 1866. Pen and ink, 15.9 × 11.7 cm ($6\frac{1}{4}$ × $4\frac{5}{8}$ in). By courtesy of Birmingham Museums and Art Gallery.

75 Robert Anning Bell, *Mary Magdalene*, 1903. Gesso, one of seven panels, each panel 137 × 50 cm (54 × 20 in). Fischer Fine Art Limited, London.

76 Anthony Frederick Sandys, *Mary Magdalene*, 1858–60. Oil on panel, 33.6 × 27.9 cm ($13\frac{1}{4}$ × 11 in). Delaware Art Museum, Samuel and Mary R. Bancroft Memorial Collection.

77 Daniel Maclise, *Madeline After Prayer*, 1868. Oil on canvas, 127 × 101 cm (50 × $39\frac{3}{4}$ in). National Museums and Galleries on Merseyside (Walker Art Gallery).

78 Elizabeth Siddal, *Clerk Saunders*, *c.* 1854–7. Pencil drawing, 11.4 × 8.3 cm ($4\frac{1}{2}$ × $3\frac{1}{4}$ in). Ashmolean Museum, Oxford.

79 Arthur Hughes, *The Brave Geraint (Geraint and Enid)*, 1860. Oil on canvas, 23 × 36 cm (9 × 14 in). Private Collection.

80 Julia Margaret Cameron, *Gareth and Lynette*, 1874. Photograph. National Portrait Gallery, London.

81 Julia Margaret Cameron, *And Enid Sang*, 1874. Photograph. The Royal Photographic Society, Bath.

82 Elizabeth Siddal, *Lady Affixing a Pennon to a Knight's Spear*, *c.* 1858. Watercolour, 14.3 × 14.1 cm ($5\frac{5}{8}$ × $5\frac{1}{2}$ in). Tate Gallery, London.

83 Dante Gabriel Rossetti, *Before the Battle*, 1858. Watercolour, 42.2 × 27.9 cm ($16\frac{5}{8}$ × 11 in). Courtesy, Museum of Fine Arts, Boston: Special Picture Fund.

84 William Holman Hunt, *Godiva*, 1856. Engraving for Moxon edition of Tennyson (photo: The British Library).

85 William Morris, *La Belle Iseult*, 1858. Oil on canvas, 71 × 50 cm ($28\frac{1}{8}$ × 20 in). Tate Gallery, London.

86 Jane Morris and Elizabeth Burden, *Hippolyta*, *c.* 1880. Embroidery on serge, 143.5 × 71.1 cm ($56\frac{1}{2}$ × 28 in). From the Castle Howard Collection, York.

87 William Morris (Morris and Co.), *The Recognition of Sir Tristram*, 1862. Stained-glass panel, 68 × 60.5 cm ($26\frac{3}{4}$ × $23\frac{3}{4}$ in). Bradford Art Galleries and Museums.

88 Edward Burne-Jones, *The Arming and Departure of the Knights of the Round Table on the Quest of the Holy Grail*, *c.* 1890. Tapestry; wool and silk on cotton warp, 244 × 360 cm (96 × 138 in). By courtesy of Birmingham Museums and Art Gallery.

89 John Everett Millais, *The Knight Errant*, 1870. Oil on canvas, 184.1 × 135.3 cm ($72\frac{1}{2}$ × $53\frac{1}{4}$ in). Tate Gallery, London.

90 Frank Dicksee, *Chivalry*, 1885. Oil on canvas, 183 × 136 cm (72 × $53\frac{1}{2}$ in). The Forbes Magazine Collection, New York (photo: A. C. Cooper).

91 Edward Burne-Jones, *The Beguiling of Merlin*, 1874. Oil on canvas, 186 × 111 cm (73 × $43\frac{3}{4}$ in). National Museums and Galleries on Merseyside (Lady Lever Art Gallery).

92 Elizabeth Siddal, *Sister Helen*, *c.* 1854. Pencil, 12.8 × 16 cm (5 × 6 in). Ashmolean Museum, Oxford.

93 Edward Burne-Jones, *Clara von Bork*, 1860. Watercolour with bodycolour, 34 × 18 cm ($13\frac{1}{4}$ × 7 in). Tate Gallery, London.

94 Edward Burne-Jones, *Sidonia von Bork*, 1860. Watercolour with bodycolour, 33 × 17 cm (13 × $6\frac{3}{4}$ in). Tate Gallery, London.

95 Edward Burne-Jones, *Head of Nimuë* for *The Beguiling of Merlin*, 1873. Gouache, 76.2 × 50.8 cm (30 × 20 in). Delaware Art Museum, Samuel and Mary. R. Bancroft Memorial Collection.

96 Edward Burne-Jones, *Caricature of Maria Zambaco and Self*, *c.* 1870. Pencil, 11 × 15 cm ($4\frac{1}{4}$ × 6 in). Private Collection (photo: Sotheby's, London).

97 Edward Burne-Jones, *Laus Veneris*, 1869. Oil with gold paint on canvas, 122 × 183 cm (48 × 72 in). From the collection at the Laing Art Gallery, Newcastle upon Tyne. Reproduced by permission of Tyne and Wear Museums Service.

98 Anthony Frederick Sandys, *Medea*, 1868. Oil on panel, 62.3 × 46.3 cm ($24\frac{1}{2}$ × $18\frac{1}{4}$ in). By courtesy of Birmingham Museums and Art Gallery.

99 John William Waterhouse, *The Magic Circle*, 1886. Oil, 182.9 × 127 cm (72 × 50 in). Tate Gallery, London.

100 Anthony Frederick Sandys, *Medusa*, 1875. Chalk, 72.7 × 54.6 cm ($28\frac{5}{8}$ × $21\frac{1}{2}$ in). By courtesy of the Board of Trustees of the Victoria and Albert Museum, London.

101 John William Waterhouse, *La Belle Dame Sans Merci*, 1893. Oil on canvas, 112 × 81 cm (44 × 32 in). Hessisches Landesmuseum, Darmstadt.

102 Evelyn de Morgan, *Queen Eleanor and Fair Rosamund*, *c.* 1888. Oil on canvas, 73.6 × 64.7 cm (29 × $25\frac{1}{2}$ in). The de Morgan Foundation, London (photo: Bridgeman Art Library).

103 Dante Gabriel Rossetti, *Monna Vanna*, 1866. Oil on canvas, 88.9 × 86.4 cm (35 × 34 in). Tate Gallery, London.

104 William Holman Hunt, *The Afterglow in Egypt*, 1854–63. Oil on canvas, 185.4 × 86.3 cm (73 × 34 in). Southampton City Art Gallery and Museum.

105 Edward Burne-Jones, *Hope* (unfinished), 1861–2. Oil, 49.5 × 38 cm ($19\frac{1}{2}$ × 15 in). Private Collection (photo: Bridgeman Art Library).

106 Edward Burne-Jones, *Winter*, 1869. Gouache, 122.5 × 45 cm ($48\frac{1}{4}$ × $17\frac{3}{4}$in). Roy Miles Gallery, London (photo: Bridgeman Art Library).

107 Edward Burne-Jones, *Summer*, 1870. Gouache, 122.5 × 45 cm ($48\frac{3}{4}$ × $17\frac{3}{4}$ in). Roy Miles Gallery, London (photo: Bridgeman Art Library).

108 Marie Spartali Stillman, *Convent Lily*, 1891. Watercolour, 45 × 36 cm (18 × 14 in). Ashmolean Museum, Oxford.

109 Julia Margaret Cameron, *Mnemosyne*, 1868. Photograph. Sotheby's, London.

110 Dante Gabriel Rossetti, *Astarte Syriaca*. Oil on canvas, 182.9 × 106.7 cm (72 × 42 in). City of Manchester Art Galleries.

111 Edward Burne-Jones, *Rossetti Carrying Cushions for a Startled Janey Morris*, *c.* 1870. Pencil, 18 × 11.4 cm (7 × $4\frac{1}{2}$ in). Private Collection (photo: Sotheby's, London).

112 Dante Gabriel Rossetti, *The Day Dream*, 1880. Oil on canvas, 158.7 × 92.7 cm ($62\frac{1}{2}$ × $36\frac{1}{2}$ in). By courtesy of the Board of Trustees of the Victoria and Albert Museum, London.

113 Evelyn de Morgan, *The Hour Glass*, 1904–5. Oil on canvas, 92.7 × 78.7 cm ($36\frac{1}{2}$ × 31 in). The de Morgan Foundation, London (photo: Bridgeman Art Library).

114 Evelyn de Morgan, study of the head of Jane Morris in old age for the painting *The Hour Glass*, *c.* 1904. The de Morgan Foundation, London (photo: William Morris Gallery).

115 Kate Elizabeth Bunce, *Melody* (*Musica*), date unknown. Oil on canvas, 74.9 × 49.5 cm ($29\frac{1}{2}$ × $19\frac{1}{2}$ in). By courtesy of Birmingham Museums and Art Gallery.

116 Dante Gabriel Rossetti, *Beata Beatrix*, *c.* 1864–70. Oil on canvas, 86.4 × 66 cm (34 × 26 in). Tate Gallery, London.

117 John Everett Millais, *Ophelia*, 1852. Oil on canvas, 76.2 × 111.8 cm (30 × 44 in). Tate Gallery, London.

118 Arthur Hughes, *Ophelia*, 1852. Oil on canvas, 69 × 124 cm (27 × $48\frac{3}{4}$ in). City of Manchester Art Galleries.

119 Dante Gabriel Rossetti, *How They Met Themselves 1851–60*, 1860. Pen and ink and wash on paper, 26.9 × 21.2 cm ($10\frac{1}{2}$ × $8\frac{1}{4}$ in). Fitzwilliam Museum, Cambridge.

120 Dante Gabriel Rossetti, *Elizabeth Rossetti*, *c.* 1861. Painted photograph, 7.6 × 5.4 cm (3 × 2 in) with gold frame with jade, opal, diamond and sapphire. Walters Art Gallery, Baltimore.

121 William Holman Hunt, *Isabella and the Pot of Basil*, 1876. Oil on canvas, 187 × 116 cm ($73\frac{1}{2}$ × $45\frac{1}{2}$ in). From the collection at the Laing Art Gallery, Newcastle upon Tyne. Reproduced by permission of Tyne and Wear Museums Service.

122 William Holman Hunt, *Fanny Holman Hunt*, 1866–8. Oil on canvas, 104 × 73 cm (41 × $28\frac{3}{4}$ in). The Toledo Museum of Art, Ohio: Gift of Edward Drummond Libbey.

123 Dante Gabriel Rossetti, *Proserpine*, 1873–7. Oil on canvas, 119.5 × 57.8 cm (42 × 22 in). Tate Gallery, London.

124 Dante Gabriel Rossetti, *La Pia de'Tolomei*, 1868–80. Oil on canvas, 105.4 × 120.6 cm (41 × $47\frac{1}{2}$ in). Spencer Museum of Art, University of Kansas, Lawrence, Kansas.

125 Julia Margaret Cameron. *Call, I follow, I follow – let me die*, 1867. Photograph. The Royal Photographic Society, Bath.

126 John William Waterhouse, *'I am Half Sick of Shadows' said the Lady of Shalott*, 1915. Oil on canvas, 100.3 × 73.7 cm ($39\frac{1}{2}$ × 29 in). Art Gallery of Ontario, Toronto. Gift of Mrs Phillip B. Jackson, 1971.

127 William Holman Hunt, *The Lady of Shalott*, 1857. Engraving for Moxon edition of Tennyson.

128 William Maw Egley, *The Lady of Shalott*, 1858. Oil on canvas, 61 × 73.7 cm (24 × 29 in). Sheffield City Art Galleries.

129 Evelyn de Morgan, *The Captives*, *c.* 1888. Oil on canvas, 55.8 × 83.8 cm (22 × 33 in). The de Morgan Foundation, London (photo: Bridgeman Art Library).

130 Evelyn de Morgan, *The Gilded Cage*, 1919. Oil on canvas, 89.5 × 106.6 cm ($35\frac{1}{4}$ × 42 in). The de Morgan Foundation, London (photo: Bridgeman Art Library).

Select Bibliography

The literature of and about Pre-Raphaelitism is extensive and ever-growing. For a full list of books and articles published before 1965, see W. A. Fredeman, *Pre-Raphaelitism: A Bibliocritical Study*, London and Cambridge, Mass. 1965.

Bartram, Michael, *Pre-Raphaelite Photography*, British Council exhibition catalogue, London 1983.
Bartram, Michael, *The Pre-Raphaelite Camera: Aspects of Victorian Photography*, London 1985.
Banham, Joanna and Harris, Jennifer, eds. *William Morris and the Middle Ages*, Manchester University exhibition catalogue, 1984.
Baum, P. F., ed. *Dante Gabriel Rossetti's Letters to Fanny Cornforth*, Baltimore 1940.
Brown University, *Ladies of Shalott: A Victorian Masterpiece and Its Contexts*, exhibition catalogue, Providence, Rhode Island 1985.
Bryson, John, ed. *Dante Gabriel Rossetti and Jane Morris: Their Correspondence*, Oxford 1976.
Burne-Jones, Georgiana, *Memorials of Edward Burne-Jones*, 2 vols, London 1904.

Casteras, Susan P., *The Substance or the Shadow: Images of Victorian Womanhood*, Yale Center for British Art exhibition catalogue, New Haven 1982.
Christian, John, *Burne-Jones*, Arts Council of Great Britain exhibition catalogue, London 1975.
Christian, John, *Symbolists and Decadents*, London 1977.

Doughty, O. and Wahl, J. R., eds. *Letters of Dante Gabriel Rossetti*, 4 vols, Oxford and New York 1965–7.
Dufty, A. R., *Morris Embroideries: the Prototypes*, London 1985.

Fredeman, W. E., ed. *The Pre-Raphaelite Brotherhood Journal 1849–1853*, London 1975.
Fitzgerald, Penelope, *Edward Burne-Jones*, London 1979.

Geffrye Museum, *Solomon: A Family of Painters*, exhibition catalogue, London 1985.
Girouard, Mark, *The Return to Camelot: Chivalry and the English Gentleman*, New Haven and London 1981.
Grieve, A. I., *The Art of Dante Gabriel Rossetti*, 3 vols, Norwich 1973–8.

Harrison, Martin and Waters, Bill, *Burne-Jones*, London 1973.
Hobson, Anthony, *The Art and Life of J. W. Waterhouse 1849–1917*, London 1980.
Hopkinson, Amanda, *Julia Margaret Cameron*, London 1986.
Hunt, W. H., *Pre-Raphaelitism and the Pre-Raphaelite Brotherhood*, 2 vols, London 1905, repr. New York 1967.

Lutyens, Mary, *Millais and the Ruskins*, London 1967.

Marsh, Jan, *Pre-Raphaelite Sisterhood*, London and New York 1985.
Marsh, Jan, *Jane and May Morris*, London 1986.
Millais, Geoffrey, *Sir John Everett Millais*, London 1979.
Millais, J. G., ed. *John Everett Millais: Life and Letters*, 2 vols, London 1899.
Mullins, Edwin, *The Painted Witch: Female Body, Male Art*, London 1985.

Nicoll, John, *The Pre-Raphaelites*, London 1970.
Nunn, Pamela Gerrish, *Canvassing: Recollections by Six Victorian Women Artists*, London 1986.

Parris, Leslie, ed. *Pre-Raphaelite Papers*, London 1984.
Parry, Linda, *William Morris Textiles*, London 1983.
Pre-Raphaelite Illustrations from Moxon's Tennyson, Academy Editions, London 1978.

Rose, Andrea, *Pre-Raphaelite Portraits*, Oxford 1981.
Rossetti, W. M., 'Elizabeth Eleanor Siddal', *Burlington Magazine*, May 1903.
Ruskin, John, *Collected Works*, ed. E. T. Cooke and A. D. Wedderburn, 37 vols, London 1903–12.
Ruskin, John, *Sesame and Lilies*, London 1871.

Siddal, Elizabeth, *Poems and Drawings*, ed. R. C. Lewis and M. S. Lasner, Wolfille, Nova Scotia 1978.
Surtees, Virginia, ed. *The Paintings and Drawings of Dante Gabriel Rossetti: A Catalogue Raisonné*, 2 vols, Oxford and New York 1971.
Surtees, Virginia, ed. *The Diaries of George Price Boyce*, London 1980.
Surtees, Virginia, ed. *The Diary of Ford Madox Brown*, New Haven and London 1981.

Tate Gallery, *The Pre-Raphaelites*, exhibition catalogue, London 1984.

Wood, Christopher, *The Pre-Raphaelites*, London 1981.
Wood, Christopher, *Victorian Panorama: Paintings of Victorian Life*, London 1976.

Index